Physical Characteristics of Hovawart

(from the Fédération Cynologique Internationale's breed standard)

Body: *Back:* Straight and firm. *Loin:* Solid, a little longer than the rump. *Croup:* Slightly inclined and of medium length. *Chest:* Broad, slopes well and is strong.

Color: The Hovawart comes in three colors: black, black and gold and blonde. The eyelids, lips and paws are black.

Hindquarters: Seen from the rear, the back limbs are solid and well balanced and angled. *Thigh and leg:* Very good muscles. *Hock joint:* Powerful and well formed.

Size: Height at the withers: Male: 63–70 cm; female: 58–65 cm.

Tail: The length of the bushy tail exceeds the hock joint without touching the ground. It hangs or curves across the back according to the dog's mood.

Feet: Rounded, strong and compact. The toes are arched and tight. Except in countries that forbid the practice, the dewclaws should be removed.

Hovawart

◇

By Francis Dedier and Viviana Pavan

Contents

Health Care of Your Hovawart   105

Discover how to select a qualified vet and care for your dog at all stages of life. Topics include vaccinations, skin problems, dealing with external and internal parasites and common medical and behavioral conditions.

Your Senior Hovawart   136

Consider the care of your senior Hovawart, including the proper diet for a senior. Recognize the signs of an aging dog, both behavioral and medical; implement a special-care program with your vet and become comfortable with making the final decisions and arrangements for your senior Hovawart.

Showing Your Hovawart   142

Experience the dog show world by becoming acquainted with how conformation shows are organized and the basics of handling. Also learn about the Fédération Cynologique Internationale, the world's international kennel club.

Behavior of Your Hovawart   146

Learn to recognize and handle behavioral problems that may arise with your Hovawart. Topics discussed include separation anxiety, aggression, barking, chewing, digging, begging, jumping up, etc.

KENNEL CLUB BOOKS: **HOVAWART**
ISBN: 1-59378-377-9

Copyright © 2003 Kennel Club Books, Inc.
308 Main Street, Allenhurst, NJ 07711 USA
Cover Design Patented: US 6,435,559 B2 • Printed in South Korea

Photos by Norvia Behling, T. J. Calhoun, Carolina Biological Supply, Francis Dedier, Doskocil, Isabelle Francais, James Hayden-Yoav, Carol Ann Johnson, Bill Jonas, Dwight R. Kuhn, Dr. Dennis Kunkel, Viviana Pavan, Mikki Pet Products, Phototake, Jean Claude Revy, Alex Smith, Dr. Andrew Spielman and Alice van Kempen.

The publisher wishes to thank all of the owners of the dogs featured in this book, including Koftemme Burkhard, Mr. Burr, Mr. Cordonnier, the Dedier family, Mr. Descamps, Mrs. Duhayer, Mr. Josef Hardegger, Mrs. Min Inches, Mr. Koninx, Maria Kuncewicz, Mrs. Lecander, Jeff Lipp, the Van Mixo-DeWeerdt family, the Pavan family, Miss Piecznyska, Mr. Piels-Wanceslow, Mr. Romain, the Robotham family, Michel Roy, Mrs. Sant, Miss Annie Stewart, Mr. Volle, Anja Weber, Lothar Wernicke and Mr. Wrancken.

Illustrations by Patricia Peters.

A champion from the breed's homeland, this is German Ch. Aldo vom Buvagt-Hus, owned by Lothar Wernicke.

A mountain Molosser, the Hovawart—as with most large dogs—is descended from the ancient Tibetan Mastiff, which emerged in the third century. Nonetheless, its history remained practically unknown until the Middle Ages.

ORIGIN AND DEVELOPMENT IN GERMANY

The name "Hovawart" finds its origins in Middle Ages High German, taken from *Hofewart*, meaning the guardian of a farm or estate. At that time, most large dogs were used to guard land and property, as well as protect herds from predators such as wolves. As with other breeds, the gradual disappearance of these predators brought about an interest in the dog itself, and a young guard dog from such a farm was undeniably the basis for the modern Hovawart.

Documentation of the Hovawart dates back as far as the 13th century, with one of the earliest accounts telling of the dog's bravery while his family's estate was being pillaged. In another early record, an engraving

by Albrecht Dürer, dated 1513 and entitled *The Chevalier, Death and the Devil*, we see a man mounted on a horse, showing no fear in the face of death and the devil. Alongside him is a dog that very much resembles a Hovawart.

With the rise of other breeds, which apparently were considered more "fashionable" at the time, interest in the Hovawart unfortunately waned. At the turn of the 20th century, very few of these dogs remained. Then, in the early 20th century, shortly after World War I, the renowned cynologist K. F. König attempted to recreate the Hovawart as it existed in the Middle Ages, with its very specific character, working qualities and ability to serve as a guardian. He sought to recreate the essential characteristics of a robust and resistant dog with a strong constitution and a nobility of movement. A man of strong character, König steered the development of the breed with the firm hand of one who loves his work. He edited a book on the recreation of the Hovawart and, as of 1922, took on complete responsibility for promoting the breed in Germany.

There are two opposing theories regarding the revitalization of the Hovawart breed. One theory purports that today's Hovawart is based on pure descendants of the original dogs, which were found existing in the Black Forest long after the decline of the breed. The other theory states that the breed was in fact reconstructed, using breeds such as the German Shepherd Dog, Kuvasz, Leonberger, Newfoundland and perhaps others. Nonetheless, type was established rather quickly, being set in the first half of the 20th century.

GENUS *CANIS*

Dogs and wolves are members of the genus *Canis*. Wolves are known scientifically as *Canis lupus* while dogs are known as *Canis domesticus*. Dogs and wolves are known to interbreed. The term "canine" derives from the Latin-derived word *Canis*. The term "dog" has no scientific basis but has been used for thousands of years. The origin of the word "dog" has never been authoritatively ascertained.

In 1937, the German Kennel Club—to the pride of those who had pioneered the Hovawart—officially recognized the breed. World War II, however, brought about the near-extinction of the Hovawart, a situation faced by most breeds of dog at that time. Shortly afterwards, in 1947, some tenacious breeders—principally from the region of Hesse—rekindled interest and publicity surrounding the Hovawart.

In 1964, the Fédération Cynologique Internationale (FCI), the governing canine organization in continental Europe, recognized the Hovawart as a working breed. The breed is classified in the FCI's Group 2 (Pinscher and Schnauzer type, Molossian and Swiss

The group of breeds known as Molossers, in which the Hovawart is included, stems from ancient dogs that were identified as *Canis molossus*.

Mountain and Cattledogs), Section 2 (Molossian, Mountain type), with working trial.

The following year, 1965, the Rassezuchtverein für Hovawart-Hunde (RZV) was formed with the purpose of controlling and promoting the breed. One of the German club's main goals was to eliminate any genetic imperfections, such as hip dysplasia,

through strictly regulating breeding. The RZV also developed what was to become the international Hovawart breed standard, that which is accepted and recognized by the FCI.

THE BREED OUTSIDE ITS HOMELAND
Little by little, other countries fell into step behind the Germans. Important breeders emerged in the Netherlands, Switzerland and Austria. In France, serious breeding began in 1990, with Scandinavia, Great Britain, Belgium and Italy not far behind. Other countries, such as the Czech Republic, Hungary and Poland, as well as the United

Hovawarts in the breed's three recognized colors: black and gold, blonde and solid black.

Asko von Frohnauer Feld, owned by Mr. Burr, shows the desired natural characteristics of the modern Hovawart, reminiscent of its rustic early ancestors.

A Hovawart from the Netherlands, a country in which there is a growing breed following.

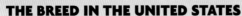

THE BREED IN THE UNITED STATES

The Hovawart is considered a rare breed in the United States, with relatively low numbers of the breed in the country. Nonetheless, interest in the breed is growing, and Hovawart breeders and fanciers are working to promote the breed in the US through several national clubs. Although not currently recognized by the American Kennel Club, the main canine governing body in the country, the Hovawart is recognized by the United Kennel Club and the American Rare Breed Association (ARBA). Hovawarts compete in ARBA shows under the breed standard of their homeland, Germany, which is that accepted by the Fédération Cynologique Internationale.

THE BREED IN THE UK

Min Inches is the pioneer of the Hovawart in the United Kingdom. She is responsible for the first imports into the country and for lobbying to England's Kennel Club for breed recognition. Her efforts paid off, as the Hovawart Club of Great Britain, founded in 1982, is a member of the Kennel Club, and the breed's Interim standard is also accepted by the KC. The Hovawart Club of Great Britain is currently an Associate Member of the International Hovawart Federation. The breed has established a foothold in the UK, and its future looks bright!

States and Canada, are progressively opening up to breeding.

Member clubs from countries around the world are united under a common association, the International Hovawart Federation, established in 1984. The goals of this organization are to standardize breeding on an international level and create a rich donor bank from which the best subjects may be taken for reproduction. So, although considered a rare breed in most countries, the Hovawart does have dedicated people promoting its best interests wherever the breed is found.

Though a rare breed in the UK, the Hovawart has a firm foothold there, as illustrated by this lovely British example.

The Hovawart's instinctive guarding nature is not lost in the home environment. Pet Hovawarts are vigilant sentinels of "their" property.

CHARACTERISTICS OF THE

HOVAWART

A medium-sized dog, the Hovawart should not be large or heavy, but supple in his movements while retaining his strength. Very attached to his owners, the Hovawart is an excellent and long-lived family dog, which, under careful, serious training can also prove to be a very useful animal. He will defend his family under any circumstances, establishing a very close relationship with his loved ones, especially children.

Although he has a very friendly nature, the Hovawart is not easy to train. The Hovawart remains essentially rustic and tends to do what he feels like doing even when commanded otherwise, which adds to his charm but indicates a need for a good obedience school or a very skilled trainer. Although he retains a calm and very balanced temperament, the Hovawart is not a docile creature. Calm and contented yet born to play, the Hovawart exhibits an energetic and frisky nature when at liberty in the yard. The same is true in the home; you can be certain that you'll lose your slippers if you leave them out for a Hovawart puppy to find.

In her book on the Hovawart, Doris Jung indicates that the breed is "not a submissive dog, but a dog that obeys willingly without giving up his pride or becoming a slave to humans. He is a friend and comrade, not a servant."

The training of a Hovawart should begin as soon as possible, either at home or at obedience classes. This is very important, as it is the essential ardor in the young Hovawart that drives him to learn to obey and loyally follow his owner. Every dog needs a

TAKING CARE

Science is showing that as people take care of their pets, the pets are taking care of their owners. A recent study published in the *American Journal of Cardiology* found that having a pet can prolong his owner's life. Pet owners generally have lower blood pressure, and pets help their owners to relax and keep more physically fit. It was also found that pets help to keep the elderly connected to their communities.

leader in order to develop in a balanced and sound manner. Without a competent leader, the dog himself will take control, which is obviously something to avoid. This is common to every breed of dog.

A sensitive breed, the Hovawart should under no circumstances be trained harshly. The dog is not a part of an alarm system but a member of the family. The Hovawart should never be kept tied out on a lead or chain. The owner who understands these basic tenets will more fully be able to develop his relationship with his Hovawart.

The Hovawart's rapid understanding of what is expected makes him a valuable work dog, and ensures that a Hovawart will accomplish his tasks with an air of "You see? I did that for you."

However, if one day the dog does not perform as expected, he should not be forced or coerced. Rather, the exercise should be taken up again later in the form of a game.

Maria Kuncewicz, who represents the breed in France and whose bitch Loula is a prizewinner with a long career, comments, "You should be happy when your Hovawart simply gets off the sofa when you command." Although somewhat exaggerated, this humorous image of the very friendly, convivial Hovawart indicates that authority should be used with kid gloves.

The dog loves to participate in every aspect of family life—especially in relation to children—and will recognize who holds the lead. He will push his owner to burn a few calories as he strains

A Hovawart's home is his castle, and he will make himself comfortable. Despite his rustic beginnings, this is not an outdoors-only dog.

Training a Hovawart can be quite an experience, and definitely a challenge...are you ready for it?

Look at the excitement! Is there any doubt that Hovawarts love their owners?

on the lead during a walk, but should the young, old or infirm take the lead, the dog recognizes his frailty and will hold back. Regardless, all members of the family must realize that the Hovawart is a dog, not a toy.

Although not an excessive barker, this breed has an imposing voice and physique that puts fear into any intruder. As an individual, the dog is unlikely to stray far from his home or his owner, for he prefers the family unit to wandering out of sight.

The Hovawart's rural background makes it indifferent to changes in temperature or climate, although, due to its semi-long coat, the breed prefers colder climes such as that of its place of origin, Germany. If the thermometer rises, a large bowl of water should be left handy at all times for the dog. Neither rain nor wind is a problem, given the thickness of the dog's coat, and the

Hovawart loves to roll in, dig in and kick snow about like a child. The coat comes in three colors—a golden or flaxen color (blonde), solid black and black and gold.

BREED-SPECIFIC HEALTH CONCERNS
A number of illnesses exist to which the Hovawart is susceptible. All prospective owners should discuss these problems with the breeder, as responsible breeders strive to eliminate all genetic disorders through careful breeding. Also, being acquainted with the health problems, both genetic and otherwise, will help an owner be better prepared to recognize symptoms and get his Hovawart the necessary veterinary attention. The following health concerns are hereditary in nature.

Hip dysplasia is a genetic malformation of the hip joint between the head of the femur and the socket in which the femoral head rests. Very strict regulations regarding hip dysplasia and breeding are imposed by Hovawart clubs. Your dog should receive x-rays to make sure that he has no evidence of dysplasia. In most countries, there are organized schemes that focus on examining dogs, identifying dysplastic dogs and certifying dogs that are free of dysplasia. Any dog found with hip dysplasia is not to be bred, and none of a dysplastic dog's littermates should be bred.

Equally at home
on the farm......

....or in the snow,
and well suited to
both.

Clear, bright and healthy eyes can make any Hovawart smile.

Although it has a hereditary basis, hip dysplasia can be aggravated by environmental factors as well. A diet too rich in protein and too much exercise at an early age are common contributing factors to a dog's becoming dysplastic.

Hypothyroidism affects the thyroid gland by the production of too few hormones, thereby lowering the animal's metabolism. This genetic illness occurs around the age of five years. Symptoms include lack of muscle tone, loss of hair and lameness. This illness should be quickly reported to prevent further reproduction by the affected dog's parents.

Osteochondrosis results when bone cartilage does not harden as the dog grows, failing to develop into proper bone. This disease affects the shoulders, elbows, hocks and knees, making these areas fragile and injury-prone, with thickened cartilage. It appears at about six months of age, and more usually in males. Osteochondritis dissecans (OCD) can result if the cartilage becomes exposed and inflamed.

Eye problems such as entropion and ectropion can affect the Hovawart. Depending on the case, the eyelids turn in toward the eye (entropion) or turn outward and sag (ectropion), creating watery, inflamed eyes. These problems are usually hereditary but can also be contracted as a result of a wound.

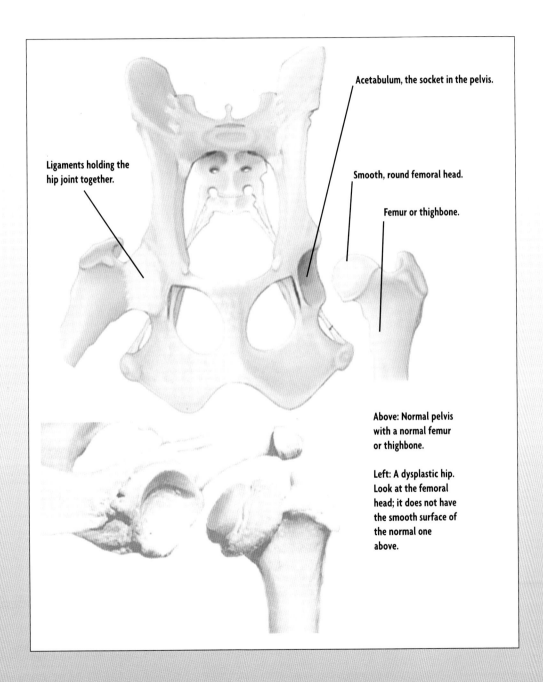

Acetabulum, the socket in the pelvis.

Ligaments holding the hip joint together.

Smooth, round femoral head.

Femur or thighbone.

Above: Normal pelvis with a normal femur or thighbone.

Left: A dysplastic hip. Look at the femoral head; it does not have the smooth surface of the normal one above.

BREED STANDARD FOR THE

HOVAWART

The breed standard presented here is the one recognized by the Fédération Cynologique Internationale (FCI) and is the standard of the breed's country of origin, Germany. The goal of any breed standard is to establish uniform characteristics, both physical and temperamental, to enable the dog to be bred in a homogenous manner and to preserve breed type. Conformation show judges also use the standard as a reference by which they pick their winners, because the dog placed first should be the dog that most closely matches the ideal set forth in the standard. The breed standard establishes the degree to which differences in the breed are tolerated because it is impossible to breed a "perfect" Hovawart, or a perfect dog of any breed for that matter. Each country has its own preferences based on the German standard, but under no circumstances may any modifications be in breach of the FCI standard.

A Hovawart in profile, showing proper structure, balance, type and substance.

Lancelot, at 13 months old, placing third in the Group at a Canadian Rare Breed Association show under American judge Marcia D. Blake-Dannaher. Owner, Michel Roy.

THE FCI STANDARD FOR THE HOVAWART

Translation by Dr J. M. Paschoud and Prof. R. Triquet

ORIGIN
Germany.

DATE OF PUBLICATION
December 1, 1998.

USE
Working breed.

FCI CLASSIFICATION
Group 2: Pinscher and Schnauzer type, Molosser and Swiss Mountain and Cattledogs. Section 2.2: Molossian, Mountain type. With working trial.

BRIEF HISTORICAL OVERVIEW
The Hovawart is a very old German race of work dog. In Middle Ages German, the name meant guardian (*Wart*) of the farm (*Hova=Hof=Farm*). Since 1922, this race has been raised based on similar-type breeds still found on farms at that time. During the first years of selective breeding, the dog was crossed with German Shepherds, Newfoundlands, Leonbergers and other breeds. The original work dog was eventually bred due to strict degrees of selection. In its country of origin, the state of health of a Hovawart is of great importance. Thus, hip dysplasia has been largely eradicated in this breed in Germany and the club hopes that similar strict breeding measures will be imitated in other countries.

GENERAL FEATURES
The Hovawart is an energetic medium-sized work dog with a relatively elongated form and long hair. The differences between the male and female are quite marked, especially in the shape of the head and overall conformation.

IMPORTANT PROPORTIONS
The length of the body measures approximately 10 to 15% more than the height at the withers.

BEHAVIOR/TEMPERAMENT
The Hovawart is a well-known multi-purpose working dog. With an even disposition and pleasant nature, it is gifted with a good instinct to protect and fight. Self-confident with a well-defined character, the dog has an average temperament. It has a very good nose. Its proportions are well balanced and its attachment to the family group makes it an excellent companion, guard dog, protector, rescuer and tracker.

HEAD
The nasal bridge is straight with its higher line parallel with that of the skull. Both the muzzle and the skull are of the same length. The head skin is tight.

CRANIAL REGION
Skull: The head is powerful and has a large, rounded forehead.
Stop: Well defined.

FACIAL REGION
Nose: The nostrils are well developed. With black and black and gold dogs, the nose color is black. With blonde dogs it is also black but can sometimes be white (snow nose).
Muzzle: Strong—seen in profile and beneath it reduces in size minimally.
Lips: Meet tightly.
Jaws/Teeth: The Hovawart jaws have a strong scissors bite and contain the usual 42 teeth. These are set square with the jaws. A pincer bite is acceptable.
Eyes: Oval, they neither protrude from nor sink into the sockets. They are medium dark brown. The eyelids fit tightly.
Ears: High-set and well-spaced, the triangular ears fall gently across the cheeks and appear to enlarge the head. In length they will at least reach the corners of the mouth. Their tip is gently rounded. When resting, they fall very flat against the cheeks. When the dog is alert, they may

Lothar Wernicke's German Ch. Aldo vom Buvagt-Hus poses with some of his many awards.

point forward somewhat. The front side of the ear is equidistant between the eye and the back of the head.

NECK
The neck is strong and of medium length. There is no dewlap.

BODY
Back: Straight and firm.

Loin: Solid, a little longer than the rump.
Croup: Slightly inclined and of medium length.
Chest: Broad, slopes well and is strong.

TAIL
The length of the bushy tail exceeds the hock joint without touching the ground. It hangs or

curves across the back according to the dog's mood.

LIMBS

Forequarters: Seen from the front and in profile, the forelegs are solid and well balanced. *Shoulders:* Well-muscled with a shoulder blade that is long and well inclined toward the rear. *Upper arm:* Long and closely fits the body. *Elbows:* Placed well together against the chest. *Pastern joint:* Strong. *Pastern:* Slightly inclined.

Hindquarters: Seen from the rear, the back limbs are solid and well balanced and angled. *Thigh and leg:* Very good muscles. *Hock joint:* Powerful and well formed.

FEET

Rounded, strong and compact. The toes are arched and tight. Except in countries that forbid the practice, the dewclaws should be removed. Black and black and gold dogs have black toenails. Blonde dogs have lighter nails.

GAIT

From every angle, the Hovawart's gait is straight, covering the ground well when at a pace. The trot extends fully with a powerful drive from the hindquarters.

SKIN

Generally well apportioned and tight. Black and black and gold dogs have a bluish hue to the

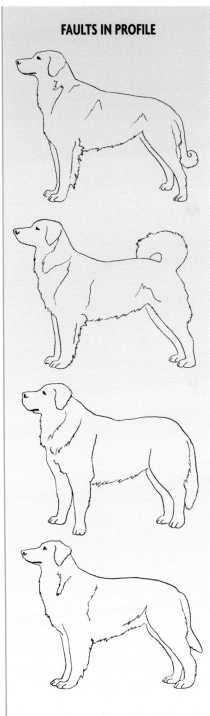

FAULTS IN PROFILE

Upright shoulders; sloping topline; weak rear that lacks angulation; too high on leg; generally lacking substance; incorrect tail with curled tip.

Upright shoulders; soft topline; low on leg; lacking angulation behind; incorrect ring tail.

Heavy-headed with excessive dewlap; loaded shoulders; toes out in front; high in rear; weak, cow-hocked behind.

Snipey muzzle; high ear-set; upright shoulders; flat feet; weak pasterns; generally lacking substance; tail too short.

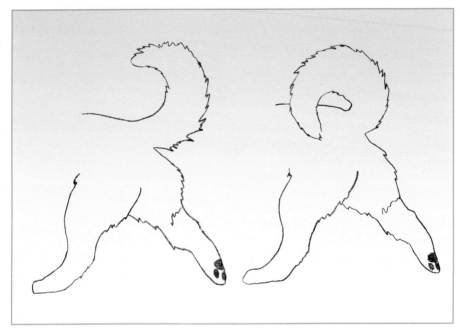

The long bushy tail should be carried straight down while the dog is standing. (Left) Correct tail carriage when moving, loosely curled over the croup. (Right) Incorrect tail carriage, in a full circle and carried to one side.

skin. Blonde-colored dogs have skin that generally has a pink sheen.

COAT

Hair: The hair is long and thick, lying close in a slightly undulating manner. There is very little undercoat. The hair is longest at the chest, along the belly, the rear legs, the thighs and the tail. It is short over the head and on the front limbs. The coat is dense.
Color: The Hovawart comes in three colors: black and gold, black, and blonde.

• *Black and Gold:* On the head, the markings begin at the base of the nose bridge, surround the corners of the mouth and

merge with the marking beneath the throat. The markings above the eyes are very visible. The marking on the chest is made up of two patches side by side that may join. Along the forelegs, the markings appear on the side, extending from the toes to the pastern and along the inside up to the elbows. The markings on the hind legs above the hock joint on the side are formed by a broad stripe that tapers along the inside almost to the belly. There is also a marking beneath the set-on of the tail. These markings are well defined and neatly drawn. Small white markings on the chest and some white hair on the toes and the end of the tail are acceptable.

French Ch. Hoffenhils Lauswart de Noir ("Dick"), owned by Miss Lecander.

A successful day for this Hovawart and handler at a show in the UK.

A black Hovawart is solid black.

A black and gold Hovawart should possess distinct markings.

Ms. Pavan's Djerda von Ascona, a handsome blonde Hovawart.

The eyelids, lips and paws are black.

• *Black:* The coat is shiny black. Small white markings along the chest and some white hair on the toes are acceptable. The eyelids, lips and paws are black.

• *Blonde:* The coat is partially blonde and shiny, gradually lightening toward the belly and the legs. Small white markings along the chest and some white hair on the toes are acceptable. The eyelids, lips and paws are black.

SIZE

Height at the withers: Male: 63–70 cm; female: 58–65 cm.

FAULTS

Every deviation from the above should be considered a fault and penalized accordingly.

Disqualifying Faults:

General

• Phenotype does not correspond to the breed.

• Females with pronounced male features.

• Males with pronounced female features.

Important Proportions

• Proportions substantially different from the standard.

Behavior/Temperament

• Aggressive, timid, lethargic or gun-shy dogs.

Natch des Trois Petits Diables at the show in which he won Best Male in the Open Class.

Head
- Absence of cranial-facial depression (stop).
- Blue eye or wall eye.
- Tipped or erect ears, rose ears or those distant from the skull.
- Wry, under- or overshot mouth.
- Absence of more than two teeth among the 4 PMI and the 2M3. Absence of any other tooth.

Neck
- Obvious dewlap or hanging throat skin.

Abdomen
- Strong sway or roach back.
- Narrow or barrel chest.
- Anomalies in the tail such as very short or pronounced tail ring.

Limbs
- Hindquarters too high.

Hair Quality
- Predominance of curls.

Color
In General:
- Any color not conforming to the standard, such as blue-gray, brown, white, patched, carbon-blonde or banded hair. Dogs marked with white patches. Some white hair on the insides of the thighs are not a disqualifying fault.

Black and Gold Dogs:
- Gray or brown patches other than the normal markings.
- Undercoat that is predominantly of another color.
- Dogs that have gray or white markings.

BREEDER'S BLUEPRINT
If you are considering breeding your bitch, it is very important that you are familiar with the breed standard. Reputable breeders breed with the intention of producing dogs that are as close as possible to the standard and that contribute to the advancement of the breed. Study the standard for both physical appearance and temperament, and make certain that your bitch and your chosen stud dog measure up.

Black Dogs:
- Those with gray or brown patches.
- Undercoat that is predominantly of another color.

Blonde Dogs:
- Some white hairs on the nose bridge is acceptable.
- General red-blonde color that does not lighten.
- Coat and ears of a blonde-white color.
- Distinct white markings.
- Dogs with dark patches or with a dark mask.

Size
- Dogs that do not reach the standard size.
- Dogs that exceed the standard size by 3 cm.

N.B. Males should have two normal testicles that fully and evenly descend into the scrotum.

HOVAWART

SELECTING A PUPPY

Good dog clubs, including national kennel clubs, Hovawart clubs and all-breed clubs can help you locate and select a reputable breeder of Hovawarts. Remember that this is a rare breed in most countries, so finding a breeder and litter will require more research and likely more travel than with a more popular breed.

You will visit with the breeder, and first impressions count—both your impression of the breeder and his of you. Choose a breeder with a strong record of producing healthy, typical, sound Hovawarts. If a litter is available, ask about the different traits of the litter's parents (appearance, work ability, behavior, health, etc.). See photos of other descendants and check that the parents are free of genetic diseases. At least the dam of the litter should be located on the breeder's premises, and, if the sire is not, you should be able to see a photo of him.

Once this labyrinth of background information has been negotiated, and the breeder deems you a worthy owner of one of his pups, you can begin to choose

ARE YOU PREPARED?

Unfortunately, when a puppy is bought by someone who does not take into consideration the time and attention that dog ownership requires, it is the puppy who suffers when he is either abandoned or placed in a shelter by a frustrated owner. So all of the "homework" you do in preparation for your pup's arrival will benefit you both. The more informed you are, the more you will know what to expect and the better equipped you will be to handle the ups and downs of raising a puppy. Hopefully, everyone in the household is willing to do his part in raising and caring for the pup. The anticipation of owning a dog often brings a lot of promises from excited family members: "I will walk him every day," "I will feed him," "I will house-train him," etc., but these things take time and effort, and promises can easily be forgotten once the novelty of the new pet has worn off.

your puppy. Gender, color and suitability of the pup's personality and ability will be large factors in your decision, and the breeder will be able to guide you in your choice.

The purchase of a Hovawart should be done conscientiously, with intelligence and with as much consideration for your family and lifestyle as for the dog itself. The dog's love of children will not be instilled without the right education. If the animal finds himself in an environment that makes him nervous, he will take a position of authority or fear, which will be difficult to correct and can lead to aggression. For example, a puppy should never be given as a Christmas gift to a child. This is usually an impulsive purchase, and the hustle and bustle of the holidays is not a good atmosphere in which to introduce a puppy.

A rational and balanced environment, in which the dog will have his place clearly designated by his owners, will enable the dog to develop the stable, affectionate temperament expected of him. In short, the Hovawart will be the ideal family friend if gently taught respect for authority. The acquisition of a Hovawart assumes some basic rules, which we will address here.

For a family that has no experience with dogs, it is advised to choose a female Hovawart, which

Are you ready for a handful of Hovawart joy? This young pup is still too young to leave the breeder and his dam.

will be easier to train, develop a maternal instinct and will be an excellent guard dog without being as dominant as the male. This is a generalization, of course, and the dog's individual personality must be considered. There is a size difference between the genders, too, with the female weighing between 70.5–77 lb (32–35 kg) and the male between 88–99 lb (40–45 kg). The male is stronger and more majestic and develops a more imposing physique that gives the impression of a more solid animal.

Once the choice of gender is made, it is important to reflect on

HANDLE WITH CARE

You should be extremely careful about handling tiny puppies. Not that you might hurt them, but that the pups' mother may exhibit what is called "maternal aggression." It is a natural, instinctive reaction for the dam to protect her young against anything she interprets as predatory or possibly harmful to her pups. The sweetest, most gentle of bitches, after whelping a litter, often reacts this way, even to her owner.

A word of advice: When handling a puppy of any age, you should always avoid taking him by his front paws.

what you expect of the new addition to the family. Do you want your Hovawart to be "simply" a family companion and good guard dog, or do you want to develop and explore his qualities as a working dog? Do you want to exhibit your friend in shows? What are you capable of providing in the way of your time, outings, training and the like?

Once these different questions have been answered, the breeder can guide you to a suitable pup or several from which to choose. If you are choosing among several pups, you may have a color preference that sways your decision. Then, it remains only to choose a name for your new companion.

Once you've made all of these important decisions, take your chosen pup in your arms and give him a big hug!

COMMITMENT OF OWNERSHIP

You have chosen the Hovawart, which means that you have decided which characteristics you want in a dog and what type of dog will best fit into your family and lifestyle. If you have selected a breeder, you have gone a step further—you have done your research and found a responsible, conscientious person who breeds quality Hovawarts and who should be a reliable source of help as you and your puppy adjust to life together. If you have observed a litter in action, you have obtained a first-hand look at the dynamics of a puppy "pack" and, thus, you have learned about each pup's individual personality—perhaps you have even found one that particularly appeals to you.

However, even if you have not yet found the Hovawart puppy of your dreams, observing pups will help you learn to recognize certain behavior and to determine what a pup's behavior indicates about his temperament. You will be able to pick out which pups are the leaders, which ones are less outgoing, which ones are confident, shy, playful, friendly, aggressive, etc. Equally as important, you will learn to recognize what a healthy pup should look and act like. All of these things will help you in your search, and when you find the Hovawart that was meant for you, you will know it!

Researching your breed, selecting a responsible breeder and observing as many pups as possible are all important steps on the way to dog ownership. It may seem like a lot of effort...and you have not even taken the pup home yet! Remember, though, you cannot be too careful when it comes to deciding on the type of dog you want and finding out about your prospective pup's background. Buying a puppy is not—or *should* not be—just another whimsical purchase. This is one instance in which you actually do get to choose your own

TEMPERAMENT COUNTS

Your selection of a good puppy can be determined by your needs. A show potential or a good pet? It is your choice. Every puppy, however, should be of good temperament. Although show-quality puppies are bred and raised with emphasis on physical conformation, responsible breeders strive for equally good temperament. Do not buy from a breeder who concentrates solely on physical beauty at the expense of personality.

family! You may be thinking that buying a puppy should be fun—it should not be so serious and so much work. Keep in mind that your puppy is not a cuddly stuffed toy or decorative lawn ornament; rather, he is a living

Three-week-old pups of "des Trois Petits Diables" ("three little devils") breeding sure look more like little angels!

creature that will become a real member of your family. You will come to realize that, while buying a puppy is a pleasurable and exciting endeavor, it is not something to be taken lightly. Relax…the fun will start when the pup comes home!

Always keep in mind that a puppy is nothing more than a baby in a furry disguise…a baby who is virtually helpless in a human world and who trusts his owner for fulfillment of his basic needs for survival. In addition to food, water and shelter, your pup needs care, protection, guidance and love. If you are not prepared to commit to this, then you are not prepared to own a dog.

"Wait a minute," you say. "How hard could this be? All of my neighbors own dogs and they seem to be doing just fine. Why should I have to worry about all of this?" Well, you should not

What a difference a month makes in this fast-growing breed: a three-month-old pup on the left; a two-month-old pup on the right.

PUPPY GROWTH

A Hovawart puppy weighs only a little over a pound at birth. The puppy's weight multiplies fourfold between four and six months old, and, in that same period, the puppy doubles in height.

---

worry about it; in fact, you will probably find that once your Hovawart pup gets used to his new home, he will fall into his place in the family quite naturally. However, it never hurts to emphasize the commitment of dog ownership. With some time and patience, it is really not too difficult to raise a curious and exuberant Hovawart pup to become a well-adjusted and well-mannered adult dog—a dog that could be your most loyal friend.

PREPARING PUPPY'S PLACE IN YOUR HOME

Researching your breed and finding a breeder are only two aspects of the "homework" you will have to do before taking your Hovawart puppy home. You will also have to prepare your home and family for the new addition. Much as you would prepare a nursery for a newborn baby, you will need to designate a place in your home that will be the puppy's own. How you prepare your home will depend on how much freedom the dog will be allowed. Whatever you decide, you must ensure that he has a place that he can "call his own."

When you bring your new puppy into your home, you are bringing him into what will become his home as well. Obviously, you did not buy a puppy with the intentions of catering to his every whim and allowing him to "rule the roost," but in order for a puppy to grow into a stable, well-adjusted dog, he has to feel comfortable in his surroundings. Remember, he is leaving the warmth and security of his dam and littermates, as well as the familiarity of the only place he has ever known, so it is important to make his transition as easy as possible. By preparing a place in your home for the puppy, you are making him feel as welcome as possible in a strange new place. It should not take him long to get used to it, but the sudden shock of being transplanted is somewhat

Future obedience contender R'mine de la Ferme Haudery gets an early education. Owned by Martine Dedier.

traumatic for a young pup. Imagine how a small child would feel in the same situation—that is how your puppy must be feeling. It is up to you to reassure him and to let him know, "Little friend, you are going to like it here!"

WHAT YOU SHOULD BUY

CRATE
To someone unfamiliar with the use of crates in dog training, it may seem like punishment to shut a dog in a crate, but this is not the case at all. Although all breeders do not advocate crate training, more and more breeders and trainers are recommending crates as preferred tools for pet puppies as well as show puppies.

YOUR SCHEDULE . . .
If you lead an erratic, unpredictable life, with daily or weekly changes in your work requirements, consider the problems of owning a puppy. The new puppy has to be fed regularly, socialized (loved, petted, handled, introduced to other people) and, most importantly, allowed to go outdoors for house-training. As the dog gets older, he can become more tolerant of deviations in his feeding and relief schedule.

Crates are not cruel—crates have many humane and highly effective uses in dog care and training. For example, crate training is a popular and very successful house-training method. In addition, a crate can keep your dog safe during travel and, perhaps most importantly, a crate provides your dog with a place of his own in your home. It serves as a "doggie bedroom" of sorts—your Hovawart can curl up in his crate when he wants to sleep or when he just needs a break. Many dogs sleep in their crates overnight. With soft bedding and his favorite toy, a crate becomes a cozy pseudo-den for your dog. Like his ancestors, he too will seek out the comfort and retreat of a den—you just happen to be providing him

CRATE-TRAINING TIPS

During crate training, you should partition off the section of the crate in which the pup stays. If he is given too big an area, this will hinder your training efforts. Crate training is based on the fact that a dog does not like to soil his sleeping quarters, so it is ineffective to keep a pup in an area that is so big that he can eliminate in one end and get far enough away from it to sleep. Also, you want to make the crate den-like for the dog. Blankets and a favorite toy will make the crate cozy for the small pup; as he grows, you may want to evict some of his "roommates" to make more room. It will take some coaxing at first, but be patient. Given some time to get used to it, your Hovawart will adapt to his new home-within-a-home quite nicely.

with something a little more luxurious than what his early ancestors enjoyed.

As far as purchasing a crate, the type that you buy is up to you. It will most likely be one of the two most popular types: wire or fiberglass. There are advantages and disadvantages to each type. For example, a wire crate is more open, allowing the air to flow through and affording the dog a view of what is going on around him, while a fiberglass crate is sturdier. Both can double as travel crates, providing protection for the dog in the car.

The size of the crate is another thing to consider. Puppies do not stay puppies forever—in fact, sometimes it seems as if they grow right before your eyes. A small crate may be fine for a very young Hovawart pup, but it will not do him much good for long! Unless you have the money and the inclination to buy a new crate every time your pup has a growth spurt, it is better to get one that will accommodate your dog both as a pup and at full size. A large-size crate will be necessary for a fully-grown Hovawart, who can stand from almost 23 to about 27.5 inches, depending on gender and the individual dog.

BEDDING

A soft crate pad will help the dog feel more at home, and you may also like to give him a small blanket. First, this will take the place of the leaves, twigs, etc. that the pup would use in the wild to make a den; the pup can make his own "burrow" in the crate. Although your pup is far removed from his den-making ancestors, the denning instinct is still a part of his genetic makeup.

Second, until you take your pup home, he has been sleeping amid the warmth of his dam and littermates, and while a blanket is not the same as a warm, breathing body, it still provides heat and something with which to snuggle. You will want to wash your pup's bedding frequently in case he has a potty "accident" in his crate, and replace or remove any blanket or pad that becomes ragged and starts to fall apart.

TOYS

Toys are a must for dogs of all ages, especially for curious playful pups. Puppies are the "children" of the dog world, and what child does not love toys? Chew toys provide enjoyment for both dog and owner—your dog will enjoy playing with his favorite toys, while you will enjoy the fact that they distract him from chewing on your expensive shoes and leather sofa. Puppies love to chew; in fact, chewing is a physical need for pups as they are teething, and everything looks appetizing! The full range of your possessions—from old dishrag to

that have been chewed to the point of becoming potentially dangerous.

Be careful of natural bones, which have a tendency to splinter into sharp, dangerous pieces. Also be careful of rawhide, which can turn into pieces that are easy to swallow and become a mushy mess on your carpet.

LEAD

A nylon lead is probably the best option, as it is the most resistant to puppy teeth should your pup take a liking to chewing on his lead. Of course, this is a habit that should be nipped in the bud, but, if your pup likes to chew on his lead, he has a very slim chance of being able to chew through the strong nylon. Nylon leads are also lightweight, which is good for a young Hovawart

Time for a new bed? This four-month-old has well outgrown his basket, but he doesn't seem to mind! Oriental carpet—are fair game in the eyes of a teething pup. Puppies are not all that discerning when it comes to finding something literally to "sink their teeth into"—everything tastes great!

Only the strongest, most durable toys should be offered to Hovawarts. Breeders advise owners to resist stuffed toys, because they can become de-stuffed in no time. The overly excited pup may ingest the stuffing, which is neither nutritious nor digestible.

Similarly, squeaky toys are quite popular, but must be avoided for the Hovawart. Perhaps a squeaky toy can be used as an aid in training, but not for free play. If a pup "disembowels" one of these, the small plastic squeaker inside can be dangerous if swallowed. Monitor the condition of all your pup's toys carefully and get rid of any

PET INSURANCE

Just like you can insure your car, your house and your own health, you likewise can insure your dog's health. Investigate a pet insurance policy by talking to your vet. Depending on the age of your dog, the breed and the kind of coverage you desire, your policy can be very affordable. Most policies cover accidental injuries, poisoning and thousands of medical problems and illnesses, including cancers. Some carriers also offer routine care and immunization coverage.

who is just getting used to the idea of walking on a lead. For everyday walking and safety purposes, the nylon lead is a good choice for the pup.

As your pup reaches adolescence, you will need to purchase a stronger thicker lead. You also may want to purchase a flexible lead. These leads allow you to extend the length to give the dog a broader area to explore or to shorten the length to keep the dog near you.

COLLAR

Your pup should get used to wearing a collar all the time since you will want to attach his ID tags to it; plus, you have to attach the lead to something! A lightweight nylon collar is a good choice. Make certain that the collar fits snugly enough so that the pup cannot wriggle out of it, but is loose enough so that it will not be uncomfortably tight around the pup's neck. You should be able to fit a finger between the pup's neck and the collar. It may take some time for your pup to get used to wearing the collar, but soon he will not even notice that it is there. Choke collars are made for training, but are not recommended for use with the sensitive Hovawart. This breed responds better to training methods based on positive reinforcement and encouragement.

TOYS, TOYS, TOYS!

With a big variety of dog toys available, and so many that look like they would be a lot of fun for a dog, be careful in your selection. It is amazing what a set of puppy teeth can do to an innocent-looking toy, so, obviously, safety is a major consideration. Be sure to choose the most durable products that you can find. Hard nylon bones and toys are a safe bet, and many of them are offered in different scents and flavors that will be sure to capture your dog's attention. It is always fun to play a game of fetch with your dog, and there are balls and flying discs that are specially made to withstand dog teeth.

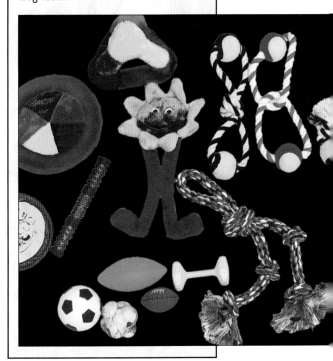

CHOOSE AN APPROPRIATE COLLAR

The **BUCKLE COLLAR** is the standard collar used for everyday purposes. Be sure that you adjust the buckle on growing puppies. Check it every day. It can become too tight overnight! These collars can be made of leather or nylon. Attach your dog's identification tags to this collar.

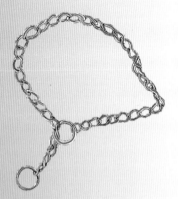

The **CHOKE COLLAR** is designed for training. It is constructed of highly polished steel so that it slides easily through the stainless steel loop. The idea is that the dog controls the pressure around his neck and he will stop pulling if the collar becomes uncomfortable.

The **HALTER** is for a trained dog that has to be restrained to prevent running away, chasing a cat and the like. Considered the most humane of all collars, it is frequently used on smaller dogs on which collars are not comfortable.

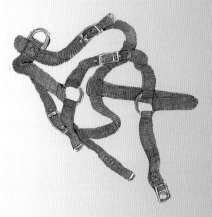

FOOD AND WATER BOWLS

Your pup will need two bowls, one for food and one for water. You may want two sets of bowls, one for indoors and one for outdoors, depending on where the dog will be fed and where he will be spending time. Stainless steel or sturdy plastic bowls are popular choices. Plastic bowls are more chewable, but dogs tend not to chew on the steel variety, which can be sterilized. It is important to buy sturdy bowls since anything is in danger of being chewed by puppy teeth and you do not want your dog to be constantly chewing apart his bowl (for his safety and for your wallet!).

As a preventative measure against deadly bloat, owners should consider it a necessity to purchase stands on which to elevate their Hovawarts' food and water bowls. Raising the bowls to the dog's level creates a more natural feeding position and decreases the risk of the dog's swallowing air, thus warding off the risk of bloat.

PHOTO COURTESY OF MIKKI PET PRODUCTS.

Purchase durable, easily cleaned bowls for your Hovawart. Stands on which to elevate the bowls are a good investment in your dog's health, as this is a preventative measure against the potentially fatal bloat.

A HEALTHY PUP
You should not even think about buying a puppy that looks sick, under-nourished, overly frightened or nervous. Sometimes a timid puppy will warm up to you after a 30-minute "let's-get-acquainted" session.

CLEANING SUPPLIES

Until a pup is house-trained, you will be doing a lot of cleaning. "Accidents" will occur, which is acceptable in the beginning stages of toilet training because the puppy does not know any better. All you can do is be prepared to clean up any accidents as soon as they happen. Old towels, paper towels, newspapers and a safe disinfectant are good to have on hand.

BEYOND THE BASICS

The items previously discussed are the bare necessities. You will find out what else you need as you go along—grooming supplies, flea/tick protection, baby gates to partition a room, etc. These things will vary depending on your situation, but it is important that you have everything you need to feed and make your Hovawart comfortable in his first few days at home.

PUPPY-PROOFING YOUR HOME

Aside from making sure that your Hovawart will be comfortable in your home, you also have to make sure that your home is safe for your Hovawart. This means taking precautions that your pup will not get into anything he should not get into and that there is nothing within his reach that may harm him should he sniff it, chew it, inspect it, etc. This probably seems obvious since, while you are primarily concerned with your pup's safety, at the same time you do not want your belongings to be ruined. Breakables should be placed out of reach. If the pup is to be limited to certain places within the house, keep any potentially dangerous items in the "off-limits" areas.

IN DUE TIME

It will take at least two weeks for your puppy to become accustomed to his new surroundings. Give him lots of love, attention, handling, frequent opportunities to relieve himself, a diet he likes to eat and a place he can call his own.

FEEDING TIPS

You will probably start feeding your pup the same food that he has been getting from the breeder; the breeder should give you a few days' supply to start you off. Although you should not give your pup too many treats, you will want to have puppy treats on hand for coaxing, training, rewards, etc. Be careful, though, as a small pup's calorie requirements are relatively low and a few treats can add up to almost a full day's worth of calories without the required nutrition.

An electrical cord can pose a danger should the puppy decide to taste it—and who is going to convince a pup that it would not make a great chew toy? Wires and cords should be fastened tightly against the wall, out of the pup's sight and away from his teeth. If your dog is going to spend time in a crate, make sure that there is nothing near his crate that he can reach if he sticks his curious little nose or paws through the openings. Just as you would with a child, keep all household cleaners and chemicals where the pup cannot reach them. Antifreeze is especially dangerous and can cause death in only small amounts; dogs are attracted to its sweet taste.

From the very first day, indicate what is and what is not allowed. For example, the pup will want to explore the bathroom, the bedrooms and other areas normally closed to animals. When this happens, firmly say "No" and lift the puppy out of the room. If he tries to enter again, repeat the exercise—the animal will very quickly understand his boundaries.

It is also important to make sure that the outside of your home is safe. Of course, your puppy should never be unsupervised, but a pup let loose in the yard will want to run and explore, and he should be granted that freedom. Do not let a fence give you a false sense of security; you would be surprised at how crafty (and persistent) a dog can be in figuring out how to dig under and squeeze his way through small holes, or to jump or climb over a fence. The remedy is to make the fence well

Make the puppy feel at home, but this is a little too close for comfort! Inviting the dog to the dinner table also triggers troublesome habits like begging and food stealing.

NATURAL TOXINS

Examine your grass and landscaping before bringing your puppy home. Many varieties of plants have leaves, stems or flowers that are toxic if ingested, and you can depend on a curious puppy to investigate them. Ask your vet for information on poisonous plants or research them at your library.

If you see your dog carrying a piece of vegetation in his mouth, approach him in a quiet, disinterested manner, avoid eye contact, pet him and gradually remove the plant from his mouth. Alternatively, offer him a treat and maybe he'll drop the plant on his own accord. Be sure no toxic plants are growing in your own yard, or kept in your home.

embedded into the ground and high enough so that it really is impossible for your dog to get over it (about 6 feet should suffice). Be sure to secure any gaps in the fence, and check the fence periodically to ensure that it is in good shape and make repairs as needed. A very determined pup may return to the same spot to "work on it" until he is able to get through.

FIRST TRIP TO THE VET

You have selected your puppy, and your home and family are ready. Now all you have to do is collect your Hovawart from the breeder and the fun begins, right? Well…not so fast. Something else you need to plan is your pup's first trip to the vet. Perhaps the breeder can recommend someone in the area with experience in Hovawarts or similar breeds, or maybe you know some other dog owners who can suggest a good vet. Either way, you should have an appointment arranged for your pup before you pick him up.

The pup's first visit will consist of an overall examination to make sure that the pup does not have any problems that are not apparent to you. The vet will also set up a schedule for the pup's vaccinations; the breeder will inform you of which ones the pup has already received and the vet can continue from there.

Puppies will appreciate soft toys for chewing when they are teething, but these toys are not made to withstand long periods of wear-and-tear. You must always supervise your Hovawart with any toy that can be chewed apart easily.

INTRODUCTION TO THE FAMILY

Everyone in the house will be excited about the puppy's coming home and will want to pet him and play with him, but it is best to make the introduction low-key so as not to overwhelm the puppy. He is apprehensive already. It is the first time he has been separated from his dam and the breeder, and the ride to your home is likely to be the first time he has been in a car. The last thing you want to do is smother him, as this will only frighten him further. This is not to say that

THE COCOA WARS

Chocolate contains the chemical thebromine, which is poisonous to dogs, although "chocolates" especially made for dogs are safe (as they don't actually contain chocolate) but not recommended. Any item that encourages your dog to enjoy the taste of cocoa should be discouraged. You should also exercise caution when using mulch in your yard and garden. This frequently contains cocoa hulls, and dogs have been known to die from eating mulch.

himself with exploring for a while. Gradually, each person should spend some time with the pup, one at a time, crouching down to get as close to the pup's level as possible, letting him sniff each person's hands and petting him gently. He definitely needs human attention and he needs to be touched—this is how to form an immediate bond. Just remember that the pup is experiencing many things for the first time, at the same time. There are new people, new noises, new smells and new things to investigate, so be gentle, be affectionate and be as comforting as you can be.

PUP'S FIRST NIGHT HOME
You have traveled home with your new charge safely in his crate. He's been to the vet for a

Let your new puppy sniff your hand to become familiar with your scent, but he doesn't have to taste you to get to know you!

human contact is not extremely necessary at this stage, because this is the time when a connection between the pup and his human family is formed. Gentle petting and soothing words should help console him, as well as just putting him down and letting him explore on his own (under your watchful eye, of course).

As soon as the dog is introduced to his new family, it is important to let him explore his new territory in peace, starting with the outside and the smells that will belong to him for the remainder of his life, and then allowing him to explore inside the house. The pup may approach the family members or may busy

PUPPY PERSONALITY
When a litter becomes available to you, choosing a pup out of all those adorable faces will not be an easy task! Sound temperament is of utmost importance, but each pup has its own personality and some may be better suited to you than others. A feisty, independent pup will do well in a home with older children and adults, while quiet, shy puppies will thrive in a home with minimal noise and distractions. Your breeder knows the pups best and should be able to guide you in the right direction.

thorough check-up; he's been weighed, his papers have been examined and perhaps he's even been vaccinated and wormed as well. He's met (and licked!) the whole family, including the excited children and the less-than-happy cat. He's explored his area, his new bed, the yard and anywhere else he's been permitted. He's eaten his first meal at home and relieved himself in the proper place. He's heard lots of new sounds, smelled new friends and seen more of the outside world than ever before...and that was just the first day! He's worn out and is ready for bed...or so you think!

It's puppy's first night home and you are ready to say "Good night." Keep in mind that this is his first night ever to be sleeping alone. The first night will very likely be a sleepless one for you. The puppy should be placed in a closed room in his crate or bed, out of reach of objects that he can chew. The room should be close to you so that you can monitor any problems during the night.

Due to the change in routine and smells (from the breeder's home to your home), the pup will no doubt cry and whine continuously. Above all, do not intervene. Do not pick the puppy up and do not seek to console him, even if his crying breaks your heart. Why? Quite simply because if you offer consolation on the first

MENTAL AND DENTAL
Toys not only help your Hovawart get the physical and mental stimulation he needs but also provide a great way to keep his teeth clean. Hard rubber or nylon toys, especially those constructed with grooves, are designed to scrape away plaque, preventing bad breath and gum infection.

INHERIT THE MIND

In order to know whether or not a puppy will fit into your lifestyle, you need to assess his personality. A good way to do this is to interact with his parents. Your pup inherits not only his appearance but also his personality and temperament from the sire and dam. If the parents are fearful or overly aggressive, these same traits may likely show up in your puppy.

night, then the pup will expect the same on the second night and will learn that if he cries, then you will come. Left alone the first night, the second night will be less traumatic and the third night will see a more reassured puppy.

Many breeders recommend placing a piece of bedding from the pup's former home in his new bed so that he recognizes and is comforted by the scent of his littermates. Others still advise placing a hot water bottle in the bed for warmth. The latter may be a good idea provided the pup doesn't attempt to suckle—he'll get good and wet, and may not fall asleep so fast.

Allowing the puppy to sleep in a bedroom is not good for the pup, because as the dog gets larger, you will find that a full-grown Hovawart will get in the way. If this happens, you will try to make the dog sleep in another room to remedy the situation. The dog will have difficulty understanding why he is no longer allowed to sleep with his master and will assume that he is being punished. From the outset, be firm and consistent in your rules. The puppy is not being deprived by having a separate sleeping area from the beginning, but is learning the important lesson of who is the boss.

PREVENTING PUPPY PROBLEMS

SOCIALIZATION

Now that you have done all of the preparatory work and have helped your pup get accustomed to his new home and family, it is about time for you to have some fun! Socializing your Hovawart pup gives you the opportunity to show off your new friend, and your pup gets to reap the benefits of being an adorable furry creature that

Three generations, showing some stages of development from puppyhood to adulthood.

people will want to pet and, in general, think is absolutely precious!

Besides getting to know his new family, your puppy should be exposed to other people, animals and situations. This will help him become well adjusted as he grows up and less prone to being timid or fearful of the new things he will encounter. Of course, he must not come into close contact with dogs you don't know well until his course of injections is fully complete.

Your pup's socialization began with the breeder, but now it is your responsibility to continue it. The socialization he receives until the age of 12 weeks is the most critical, as this is the time when he forms his impressions of the outside world. Be especially careful during the eight-to-ten-week-old period, also known as the fear period. The interaction he receives during this time should be gentle and reassuring. Lack of socialization, and/or negative experiences during the socialization period, can manifest itself in fear and aggression as the dog grows up. Your puppy needs lots of positive interaction, which of course includes human contact, affection, handling and exposure to other animals.

Once your pup has received his necessary vaccinations, feel free to take him out and about (on his lead, of course). Take him to

---

PROPER SOCIALIZATION

The socialization period for puppies is from age 8 to 16 weeks. This is the time when puppies need to leave their birth family and take up residence with their new owners, where they will meet many new people, other pets, etc. Failure to be adequately socialized can cause the dog to grow up fearing others and being shy and unfriendly due to a lack of self-confidence.

When socialized carefully from the start, children and Hovawarts make the best of friends. These two seem to see eye-to-eye...especially since they're not too far apart in height!

places where he'll experience various levels of activity—walk him around the neighborhood, take him on your daily errands, let people pet him, let him meet other dogs and pets, etc. The dog

may at first be afraid of the new situations, but do not offer consolation, as the pup will link his fear with your hugs and caresses. It is better to speak gently to the puppy, enable him to assimilate your calm with the new experiences.

As you take your young Hovawart to different places, you'll surely find that puppies do not have to try to make friends; there will be no shortage of people who will want to introduce themselves. Just make sure that you carefully supervise each meeting. If the neighborhood children want to say hello, for example, that is great—children and pups most often make great companions. However, sometimes an excited child can unintentionally handle a pup too roughly, or

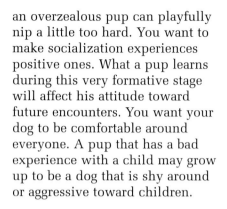

an overzealous pup can playfully nip a little too hard. You want to make socialization experiences positive ones. What a pup learns during this very formative stage will affect his attitude toward future encounters. You want your dog to be comfortable around everyone. A pup that has a bad experience with a child may grow up to be a dog that is shy around or aggressive toward children.

CONSISTENCY IN TRAINING

Dogs, being pack animals, naturally need a leader, or else they try to establish dominance in their packs. When you welcome a dog into your family, the choice of who becomes the leader and who becomes the "pack" is entirely up to you! Your pup's intuitive quest for dominance, coupled with the fact that it is nearly impossible to look at an adorable Hovawart pup with his "puppy-dog" eyes and not cave in, give the pup almost an unfair advantage in getting the upper hand!

A pup will definitely test the waters to see what he can and cannot do. Do not give in to those pleading eyes—stand your ground when it comes to disciplining the pup and make sure that all family members do the same. It will only confuse the pup if Mother tells him to get off the sofa when he is used to sitting up there with Father to watch the nightly news. Avoid discrepancies by having all

MANNERS MATTER
During the socialization process, a puppy should meet people, experience different environments and definitely be exposed to other canines. Through playing and interacting with other dogs, your puppy will learn lessons, ranging from controlling the pressure of his jaws by biting his littermates to the inner-workings of the canine pack that he will apply to his human relationships for the rest of his life. That is why removing a puppy from his litter too early (before eight weeks) can be detrimental to the pup's development.

Time for a walk, as this puppy pulls his larger friend along on the lead. Socialization between canines takes place in the form of play, friendly rough-housing and other interactions.

members of the household decide on the rules before the pup even comes home…and be consistent in enforcing them! Early training shapes the dog's personality, so you cannot be unclear in what you expect.

COMMON PUPPY PROBLEMS

The best way to prevent puppy problems is to be proactive in stopping an undesirable behavior as soon as it starts. The old saying "You can't teach an old dog new tricks" does not necessarily hold true, but it *is* true that it is much easier to discourage bad behavior in a young developing pup than to wait until the pup's bad behavior becomes the adult dog's bad habit.

There are some problems that are especially prevalent in puppies as they develop.

NIPPING

As puppies start to teethe, they feel the need to sink their teeth into anything available…unfortunately, that usually includes your fingers, arms, hair and toes. You may find this behavior cute for the first five seconds…until you feel just how sharp those puppy teeth are. Nipping is something you want to discourage immediately and consistently with a firm "No!" (or whatever number of firm "Nos" it takes for him to understand that you mean business). Then, replace your finger with an

CHEWING TIPS

Chewing goes hand in hand with nipping in the sense that a teething puppy is always looking for a way to soothe his aching gums. In this case, instead of chewing on you, he may have taken a liking to your favorite shoe or something else that he should not be chewing. Again, realize that this is a normal canine behavior that does not need to be discouraged, only redirected. Your pup just needs to be taught what is acceptable to chew on and what is off-limits. Consistently tell him "No!" when you catch him chewing on something forbidden and give him a chew toy.

Conversely, praise him when you catch him chewing on something appropriate. In this way, you are discouraging the inappropriate behavior and reinforcing the desired behavior. The puppy's chewing should stop after his adult teeth have come in, but an adult dog continues to chew for various reasons—perhaps because he is bored, needs to relieve tension or just likes to chew. That is why it is important to redirect his chewing when he is still young.

appropriate chew toy. While this behavior is merely annoying when the dog is young, it can become dangerous as your Hovawart's adult teeth grow in and his jaws develop, and he continues to think it is okay to gnaw on human appendages. Your Hovawart does not mean any harm with a friendly nip, but he also does not know his own strength.

CRYING/WHINING

Your pup will often cry, whine, whimper, howl or make some type of commotion when he is left alone. This is basically his way of calling out for attention to make sure that you know he is there and that you have not forgotten about him. Your puppy feels insecure when he is left alone, when you are out of the house and he is in his crate or when you are in another part of the house and he cannot see you. The noise he is making is an expression of the anxiety he feels at being alone, so he needs to be taught that being alone is okay. You are not actually training the dog to stop making noise; rather, you are training him to feel comfortable when he is alone and thus removing the need for him to make the noise.

This is where the crate with cozy bedding and a toy comes in handy. You want to know that your pup is safe when you are not there to supervise, and you know that he will be safe in his crate rather than roaming freely about the house. In order for the pup to stay in his crate without making a fuss, he first needs to be comfortable in his crate. On that note, it is extremely important that the crate is never used as a form of punishment; this will cause the

"Hey...one at a time!" Playing and nipping are two things that young puppies do well, and these two have started a tug-of-war with their master's sleeves.

PLAY'S THE THING

Teaching the puppy to play with his toys in running and fetching games is an ideal way to help the puppy develop muscle, learn motor skills and bond with you, his owner and master. He also needs to learn how to inhibit his bite reflex and never to use his teeth on people, forbidden objects and other animals in play. Whenever you play with your puppy, you make the rules. This becomes an important message to your puppy in teaching him that you are the pack leader and control everything he does in life. Once your dog accepts you as his leader, your relationship with him will be cemented for life.

pup to view the crate as a negative place, rather than as a place of his own for safety and retreat.

Accustom the pup to the crate in short, gradually increasing time intervals in which you put him in the crate, maybe with a treat, and stay in the room with him. If he cries or makes a fuss, do not go to him, but stay in his sight. Gradually he will realize that staying in his crate is just fine without your help, and it will not be so traumatic for him when you are not around. You may want to leave the radio on softly when you leave the house; the sound of human voices may be comforting to him.

The diet of your Hovawart puppy is something to be taken seriously. The breeder starts the litter off well, and you must follow his advice regarding how best to feed once your pup comes home with you.

HOVAWART

DIET AND FEEDING

The male Hovawart progresses in weight and height from about 17.5 pounds (8 kg) and 12 inches (30 cm) at the age of two months to around 99 pounds (45 kg) and 27.5 inches (70 cm) as an adult. The female is about the same size weight and height as the male at two months of age and progresses to around 77 pounds (35 kg) and 25.5 inches (65 cm) as an adult. Thus, the speed at which this breed grows means that special attention must be given to its diet.

Dry food products created by major dog-food manufacturers are the essential base of any nourishment, as—unlike humans—dogs do not appreciate variety in their food. They should be given the same diet every day whenever possible.

A two-month-old Hovawart should be fed about 10.5 ounces (300 grams) of food a day, progressing to about 28 ounces (800 grams) a day for a six month old. After that, the diet should be decreased to around a sensible 16–18 ounces (450–500 grams) a day for a full-grown adult.

The elevated stand brings the bowl to the dog's level. With deep-chested breeds, this is the best way to offer food and water to prevent against bloat.

In proportion, a two-month-old pup eats more than an adult. It is necessary to look at your dog's growth objectively and not give him too much food in order to prevent skeletal problems (such as back problems) and the risk of similar difficulties in the future. It is better for your pup to be slender than heavy. The pup's food should not exceed 30% protein content during the growth phase; the adult-maintenance food likely should contain less protein, depending on the dog's activity level.

It is very important to moni-tor the different elements included in the food to ascertain the percentage of protein, which should not surpass 30% for a growing puppy or an active adult. For a more passive family dog, 25% protein content will suffice. A nutritionally complete dry food is all that is necessary for your Hovawart. Any vitamin, protein or calcium supplement is *entirely unnecessary*. It serves only to improve sales of these items at the health risk of your friend.

We include here a table that describes the dietary needs of

WEANING PUPPIES

Puppies instinctively want to suck milk from their dam's teats; a normal puppy will exhibit this behavior just a few moments following birth. If puppies do not attempt to suckle within the first half-hour or so, the breeder should encourage them to do so by placing them on the nipples, having selected ones with plenty of milk. This early milk supply is important in providing the essential colostrum, which protects the puppies during the first eight to ten weeks of their lives. Although a dam's milk is much better than any commercially prepared milk formula, despite there being some excellent ones available, if the puppies do not feed, the breeder will have to feed them by hand. For those with less experience, advice from a vet is important so that not only the right quantity of milk is fed but also that of correct quality, fed at suitably frequent intervals, usually every two hours during the first few days of life.

Puppies should be allowed to nurse from their dam for about the first six weeks, although, starting around the third or fourth week, the breeder will begin to intro-duce small portions of suitable solid food. Most breeders like to introduce alternate milk and meat meals initially, building up to weaning time.

your Hovawart, including suggested amounts and ages at which to switch from a puppy to an adult diet. These suggestions should be simply taken as a guide; your breeder and vet also will be helpful in advising you about your Hovawart's diet.

WATER

Just as your dog needs proper nutrition from his food, water is an essential "nutrient" as well. Water keeps the dog's body properly hydrated and promotes normal function of the body's systems. During house-training, it is necessary to keep an eye on how much water your Hovawart is drinking,

> **AVOID STOMACH UPSET**
> Your Hovawart should never exercise right after a meal, or you run the risk of his stomach's becoming upset or of his developing bloat. You should wait at least an hour after feeding to allow the dog exercise. It is also wise to wait at least an hour after exercise before feeding the dog.

but, once he is reliably trained, he should have access to clean fresh water at all times, especially if you feed dry food only. Make certain that the dog's water bowl is clean and elevated, and change the water often.

TOO MUCH IS THE ENEMY OF WELL-BEING
(BASIC DIET FROM PUPPY TO ADULT)

AGE	2 Months	3 Months	5 Months	6 Months	9 Months	12 Months	18 Months	Adult	Active Adult or Pregnant Bitch
SUGGESTED DAILY QUANTITY	300 g	450 g	900 g	800 g	750 g	550 g	500 g	450 g	450 g
APPROX. TIME SPAN FOR 15-KG PACKAGE	1.5 months	1 month	15 days	20 days	20 days	1 month	1 month	1 month	1 month
TYPE OF FOOD	Puppy	Puppy	Puppy	Puppy	Puppy	Adult or Puppy	Adult	Adult	Extra Strength
% OF PROTEIN	28–30	28–30	28–30	28–30	28–30	25–28	25	25	30

• Feed four meals a day to three months old; three meals a day from three to six months; two meals a day from six months on.
• If the dog gets three or more hours of exercise per day, increase adult ration by 40%.
• For a pregnant bitch, feed 1.5 times the adult ration.
• It's possible to maintain the puppy on a protein-rich diet.

EXERCISE

The life of a puppy consists primarily of eating, playing, sleeping and more sleeping. For your Hovawart puppy, avoid long exhausting walks, which could damage the muscle and bone tissue. Between the ages of two and eight months, the puppy grows very quickly. It is therefore best to confine walks to two 15-minute walks each day, allowing for a period of relaxation in between. The dog may want a long walk, but will return exhausted!

After eight months of age, the walks can be extended to half an hour each. Once the dog is almost full-grown—more or less 12 months old—you can further lengthen your walks. It is a safe bet that, thereafter, it will not be the dog who is the first to tire!

All dogs require some form of exercise, regardless of breed. A sedentary lifestyle is as harmful to a dog as it is to a person. The Hovawart is a fairly active breed that enjoys exercise, but you don't have to be an Olympic athlete to provide your dog with a sufficient amount of activity!

Play sessions in the yard and letting the dog run free in the yard under your supervision also are sufficient forms of exercise for the Hovawart, as long as these are done in a securely fenced area. Fetching games can be played indoors or out; these are excellent for giving your dog active play that

DRINK, DRANK, DRUNK— MAKE IT A DOUBLE

In both humans and dogs, as well as other living organisms, water forms the major part of nearly every body tissue. Naturally, we take water for granted, but without it, life as we know it would cease.

For dogs, water is needed to keep their bodies functioning biochemically. Additionally, water is needed to replace the water lost while panting. Unlike humans, who are able to sweat to dissipate heat, dogs must pant to cool down, thereby losing the vital water that their bodies need to regulate their body temperatures. Humans lose electrolyte-containing products and other body-fluid components through sweating; dogs do not lose anything except water.

Water is essential always, but especially so when the weather is hot or humid or when your dog is exercising or working vigorously.

he will enjoy. Chasing things that move comes naturally to dogs of all breeds. When your Hovawart runs after the ball or object, praise him for picking it up and encourage him to bring it back to you for another throw. Never go to the object and pick it up yourself, or you'll soon find that you are the one retrieving the objects rather than the dog! If you choose to play games outdoors, you must have a securely fenced-in yard and/or have the dog attached to at least a 25-foot (8-meter) light line for security. You want your Hovawart to run, but not run away!

Bear in mind that an overweight dog should never be suddenly over-exercised; instead he should be encouraged to increase exercise slowly. Not only is exercise essential to keep the dog's body fit, it is essential to his mental well-being. A bored dog will find something to do, which often manifests itself in some type of destructive behavior. In this sense, exercise is essential for the owner's mental well-being as well!

GROOMING

BRUSHING AND COAT MAINTENANCE
Hovawarts are relatively easy to groom, as this is a rustic, natural breed from any point of view and should never be groomed to look otherwise. A weekly brushing is rather sufficient for the breed's

"DOES THIS COLLAR MAKE ME LOOK FAT?"
While humans may obsess about how they look and how trim their bodies are, many people believe that extra weight on their dogs is a good thing. The truth is, pets should not be over- or underweight, as both can lead to or signal sickness. In order to tell how fit your pet is, run your hands over his ribs. Are his ribs buried under a layer of fat or are they sticking out considerably? If your pet is within his normal weight range, you should be able to feel the ribs easily, but they should not protrude abnormally. If you stand above him, the outline of his body should resemble an hourglass. Some breeds do tend to be leaner while some are a bit stockier, but making sure your dog is the right weight for his breed will certainly contribute to his good health.

semi-long coat. The Hovawart's coat is a single coat, meaning that it does not have an undercoat, and this single coat is somewhat self-cleaning. This means that if you go for a walk on a rainy day and your Hovawart returns with a muddy coat, most of the dirt will fall out of the coat on its own once the dog is dry.

Regular brushing is necessary to keep the coat free of mats and tangles and to remove any dead hair in the coat. Using a comb gently where mats are prone to form is necessary as well, being extra-careful in these sensitive areas. Most Hovawarts enjoy having their coats brushed, as long as you use a gentle touch and are careful not to pull at the coat. Grooming time is a good way for dog and owner to spend time together.

Hovawarts are not significant shedders, but a little extra attention is necessary during shedding season to prevent the dead hair from matting in the coat. You can massage the dog gently by hand to remove much of the excess hair before you brush; your Hovawart should enjoy the feel of this.

BATHING

Dogs do not need to be bathed as often as humans, as too-frequent bathing will dry out the dog's skin and coat. Therefore, it is only necessary to bathe your Hovawart

A slicker brush is used to groom through the body coat.

Don't forget the neck and the chest area, where the coat is especially abundant.

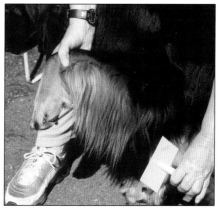

Longer furnishings, such as those on the legs, tend to mat more easily. Extra care is needed when grooming these areas.

BATHING BEAUTY

Once you are sure that the dog is thoroughly rinsed, squeeze the excess water out of his coat with your hand and dry him with a heavy towel. In cold weather, never allow your dog outside with a wet coat. There are "dry bath" products on the market, which are sprays and powders intended for spot cleaning that can be used between regular baths if necessary.

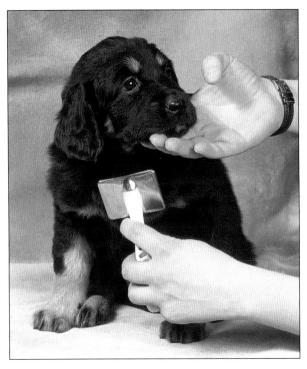

the dog. A shower or hose attachment is necessary for thoroughly wetting and rinsing the coat.

Next, apply shampoo to the dog's coat and work it into a good lather. Wash the head last, as you do not want shampoo to drip into the dog's eyes while you are washing the rest of his body. You should use only a shampoo that is made for dogs. Do not use a product made for human hair. Work the shampoo all the way down to the skin. You can use this opportunity to check the skin for any humps, bites or other abnormali-

Begin short, gentle brushing sessions with your Hovawart puppy to accustom him to being groomed.

if his coat becomes dirty or if he develops a "doggy" or otherwise unpleasant odor. If the need arises, you will want your dog to be at ease in the bath or else it could end up a wet, soapy, messy ordeal for both of you!

Brush your Hovawart thoroughly before wetting his coat. This will get rid of most mats and tangles, which are harder to remove when the coat is wet. Make certain that your dog has a good non-slip surface on which to stand. Begin by wetting the dog's coat, checking the water temperature to make sure that it is neither too hot nor too cold for

DENTAL CARE TIPS

Dry food is better for a Hovawart's teeth. You can brush your Hovawart's teeth as part of your grooming routine, but not with toothbrushes or toothpaste made for humans; use dental-care products made especially for dogs.

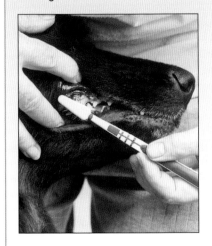

ties. Do not neglect any area of the body—get all of the hard-to-reach places.

Once the dog has been thoroughly shampooed, he requires an equally thorough rinsing. Shampoo left in the coat can be irritating to the dog's skin. Protect his eyes from the shampoo by shielding them with your hand and directing the flow of water in the opposite direction. You also should avoid getting water in the ear canal. Be prepared for your dog to shake out his coat—you might want to stand back, but make sure you have a hold on the dog to keep him from running through the house.

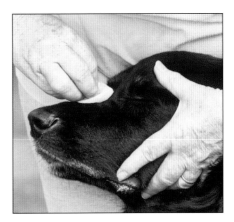

Clean the area around the eyes gently with a soft cloth or cotton ball.

EAR CLEANING

The ears should be kept clean with a piece of cotton and ear cleanser made especially for dogs. Do not probe into the ear canal with a cotton swab, as this can cause injury. Be on the lookout for any signs of infection or ear-mite infestation. If your Hovawart has been shaking his head or scratching at his ears frequently, this usually indicates a problem. If the dog's ears have an unusual odor, this is a sure sign of mite infestation or infection, and a signal to have his ears checked by the vet.

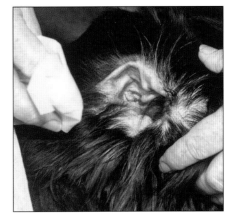

Clean the outer part of the ear carefully with a soft wipe and canine ear-cleaning powder or liquid. *Never* enter the ear canal.

NAIL CLIPPING

Your Hovawart should be accustomed to having his nails trimmed

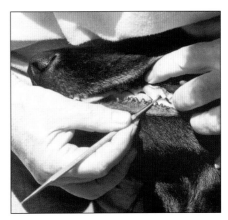

Scaling the teeth to remove tartar can be done by your vet, or your vet can teach you how to do it properly.

Nail Clipping

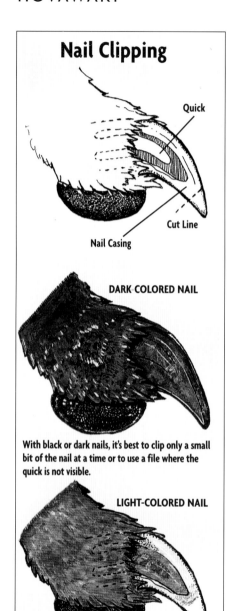

Quick

Cut Line

Nail Casing

DARK-COLORED NAIL

With black or dark nails, it's best to clip only a small bit of the nail at a time or to use a file where the quick is not visible.

LIGHT-COLORED NAIL

In light-colored nails, clipping is much simpler because you can see the vein (or quick) that grows inside the nail casing.

THE WEEKLY GRIND
You can purchase an electric tool to grind down a dog's nails rather than cut them. Some dogs don't seem to mind the electric grinder but will object strongly to nail clippers. Talking it over with your veterinarian will help you make the right choice.

at an early age since nail clipping will be part of your maintenance routine throughout his life. A dog's long nails can scratch someone unintentionally and also have a better chance of ripping and bleeding, or causing the feet to spread. A good rule of thumb is that if you can hear your dog's nails' clicking on the floor when he walks, his nails are too long.

Before you start cutting, make sure you can identify the "quick" in each nail. The quick is a blood vessel that runs through the center of each nail and grows rather close to the end. The quick will bleed if accidentally cut, which will be quite painful for the dog as it contains nerve endings. Keep some type of clotting agent on hand, such as a styptic pencil or styptic powder (the type used for shaving). This will stop the bleeding quickly when applied to the end of the cut nail. Do not panic if you cut the quick, just stop the bleeding and talk soothingly to your dog. Once he has calmed down, move on to the next nail. It is better to clip a little at a time, particularly with black-nailed dogs.

Hold your pup steady as you begin trimming his nails; you do not want him to make any sudden movements or run away. Talk to him soothingly and stroke him as you clip. Holding his foot in your hand, simply take off the end of each nail with one swift clip. You should purchase nail clippers that are made for use on dogs; you can probably find them wherever you buy pet or grooming supplies.

TRAVELING WITH YOUR HOVAWART

CAR TRAVEL

You should accustom your Hovawart to riding in a car at an early age. You may or may not take him in the car often, but at the very least he will need to go to the vet and you do not want these trips to be traumatic for the dog or troublesome for you. The safest way for a dog to ride in the car is in his crate. If he uses a crate in the house, you can use the same crate for travel.

Put the pup in the crate and see how he reacts. If he seems uneasy, you can have a passenger hold him on his lap while you drive. Other options for car travel include a specially made safety harness for dogs, which straps the dog in much like a seat belt, and partitions for the back of larger

PEDICURE TIP

A dog that spends a lot of time outside on a hard surface, such as cement or pavement, will have his nails naturally worn down and may not need to have them trimmed as often, except maybe in the colder months when he is not outside as much. Regardless, it is best to get your dog accustomed to the nail-trimming procedure at an early age so that he is used to it. Some dogs are especially sensitive about having their feet touched, but if a dog has experienced it since puppyhood, it should not bother him.

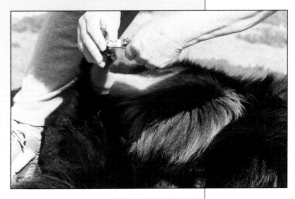

Traveling with
your Hovawart
requires the dog
to be safely
confined. This
vehicle has been
fitted with a
partition to
create a secure
area for the dog.

Traveling with your Hovawart requires the dog to be safely confined. This vehicle has been fitted with a partition to create a secure area for the dog.

vehicles to safely confine the dog. Whatever safety option you choose, *never* let the dog roam loose in the vehicle—this is very dangerous! If you should stop short, your dog can be thrown and injured. If the dog starts climbing on you and pestering you while you are driving, you will not be able to concentrate on the road. It is an unsafe situation for everyone—human and canine.

If you have a larger vehicle like a station wagon or sports utility vehicle, teach the dog to enter the car by jumping into the rear of the vehicle and not onto the seats. The puppy should also be taught from the beginning not to exit the car until commanded to do so. If car trips are only taken infrequently and are therefore not a part of the dog's normal routine,

OUTDOOR CANTEEN
When you travel with your dog, it's a good idea to take along water from home or to buy bottled water for the trip. In areas where water is sometimes chemically treated and sometimes comes right out of the ground, you can prevent adverse reactions to this essential part of your dog's diet.

then a reward once the dog exits the car is in order. Thereby, the dog will equate car trips with rewards and won't fuss.

For long trips, be prepared to stop to let the dog relieve himself, always keeping him on-lead. Take with you whatever you need to clean up after him, including paper towels and perhaps some old rags for use should he have a potty accident in the car or suffer from motion sickness. It is possible that the dog will be sick in the car. If this is a problem with your Hovawart, your vet may suggest one of the very effective homeopathic products that are used to combat motion sickness. To make your dog more comfortable when traveling on hot days, you should always leave a window cracked

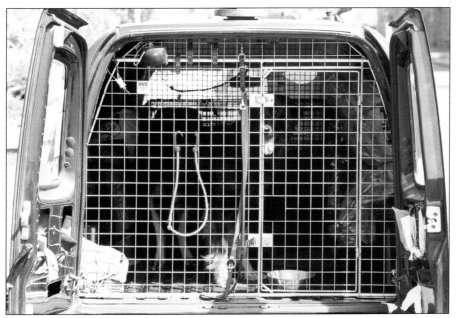

This is a similar type of partition, in which a van has been equipped with crate-like gates.

If you will need to board your dog, investigate the kennels in your area well beforehand. Be sure that the chosen kennel has spacious, clean areas for the dogs and that it is run by attentive and knowledgeable people.

open, making sure that your dog is safely confined. You should never leave your dog in the car unattended.

AIR TRAVEL

Contact your chosen airline before proceeding with your travel plans that include your Hovawart. The dog will be required to travel in a fiberglass crate and you should always check in advance with the airline regarding specific requirements for the crate's size, type and labeling. To help put the dog at ease, give him one of his favorite toys in the crate. Do not feed the dog for several hours prior to checking in so that you minimize his need to relieve himself. Some airlines require you to provide documentation of when the dog has last been fed. In any case, a light meal is best. For long trips, you will have to attach bowls and some food to the dog's crate so

that airline employees can tend to him between legs of the trip.

Make sure that your dog is properly identified and that your contact information appears on his ID tags and on his crate. Your Hovawart will travel in a different area of the plane than the human passengers, so every rule must be strictly followed to prevent the slight risk of getting separated from your dog.

VACATIONS AND BOARDING

So you want to take a family vacation—and you want to include *all* members of the family. You would probably make arrangements for accommodations ahead of time anyway, but this is especially important when traveling with a dog. You do not want to make an overnight stop at the only place around for miles, only to find out that they do not allow dogs. Also, you do not want to reserve a place for your family without confirming that you are traveling with a dog, because, if it is against the hotel's policy, you may end up without a place to stay.

Alternatively, if you are traveling and choose not to bring your Hovawart, you will have to make arrangements for him while you are away. Some options are to take him to a neighbor's house to stay while you are gone, to have a trusted neighbor stop by often or stay at your house or to bring your dog to a reputable boarding kennel. If you choose to board him at a kennel, you should visit in advance to see the facilities provided and where the dogs are kept. Are the dogs' areas spacious and kept clean? Talk to some of the employees and observe how they treat the dogs—do they spend time with the dogs, play with them, exercise them, etc.? Also find out the kennel's policy on vaccinations and what they require. This is for all of the dogs' safety, since there is a greater risk of diseases being passed from dog to dog when dogs are kept together.

IDENTIFICATION

Your Hovawart is your valued companion and friend. That is why you always keep a close eye on him and you have made sure that he cannot escape from the yard or wriggle out of his collar and run away from you. However, accidents can happen and there

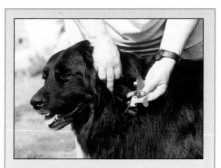

COLLAR REQUIRED

If your dog gets lost, he is not able to ask for directions home. Identification tags fastened to the collar give important information—the dog's name, the owner's name, the owner's address and a telephone number where the owner can be reached. This makes it easy for whomever finds the dog to contact the owner and arrange to have the dog returned. An added advantage is that a person will be more likely to approach a lost dog who has ID tags on his collar; it tells the person that this is somebody's pet rather than a stray. This is the easiest and fastest method of identification, provided that the tags stay on the collar and the collar stays on the dog.

may come a time when your dog unexpectedly becomes separated from you. If this unfortunate event should occur, the first thing on your mind will be finding him. Proper identification, including an ID tag and possibly a tattoo and/or microchip, will increase the chances of his being returned to you safely and quickly.

A well-behaved group, looking beautiful and posing politely.

TRAINING YOUR
HOVAWART

Living with an untrained dog is a lot like owning a piano that you do not know how to play—it is a nice object to look at, but it does not do much more than that to bring you pleasure. Now try taking piano lessons, and suddenly the piano comes alive and brings forth magical sounds and rhythms that set your heart singing and your body swaying.

The same is true with your Hovawart. Any dog is a big responsibility and, if not trained sensibly, may develop unacceptable behavior that annoys you or could even cause family friction.

To train your Hovawart, you may like to enroll in an obedience class. Teach your dog good manners as you learn how and why he behaves the way he does. Find out how to communicate with your dog and how to recognize and understand his communications with you. Suddenly the dog takes on a new role in your life—he is clever, interesting, well behaved and fun to be with. He demonstrates his bond of devotion to you daily. In other words, your Hovawart does wonders for your ego because he constantly reminds you that you are not only his leader, you are his hero!

Those involved with teaching dog obedience and counseling owners about their dogs' behavior have discovered some interesting facts about dog ownership. For example, training dogs when they are puppies results in the highest rate of success in developing well-mannered and well-adjusted adult dogs. Training an older dog, from six months to six years of age, can produce almost equal results, providing that the owner accepts the dog's slower rate of learning capability and is willing to work patiently to help the dog succeed at developing to his fullest potential. Unfortunately, many owners of untrained adult dogs lack the patience factor, so they do not persist until their dogs are successful at learning particular behaviors.

Training a puppy aged 10 to 16 weeks (20 weeks at the most) is like working with a dry sponge in a pool of water. The pup soaks up whatever you show him and constantly looks for more things to do and learn. At this early age, his body is not yet producing hormones, and therein lies the reason for such a high rate of success. Without hormones, he is focused on his owners and not particularly interested in investigating other places, dogs, people, etc. You are his leader: his provider of food, water, shelter and security. He latches onto you and wants to stay close. He will usually follow you from room to room, will not let you out of his sight when you are outdoors with him and will respond in like manner to the people and animals you encounter. If you greet a friend warmly, he will be happy to greet the person as well. If, however, you are hesitant or anxious about the approach of a complete stranger, he will respond accordingly.

Once the puppy begins to produce hormones, his natural curiosity emerges and he begins to investigate the world around him. It is at this time when you may notice that the untrained dog begins to wander away from you and even ignore your commands to stay close. When this behavior becomes a problem, you have two choices: get rid of the dog or train him. It is strongly urged that you choose the latter option.

You usually will be able to find obedience classes within a

PARENTAL GUIDANCE
Training a dog is a life experience. Many parents admit that much of what they know about raising children they learned from caring for their dogs. Dogs respond to love, fairness and guidance, just as children do. Become a good dog owner and you may become an even better parent.

reasonable distance from your home, but you can also do a lot to train your dog yourself. Sometimes there are classes available, but the tuition is too costly. Whatever the circumstances, the solution to training your dog without formal obedience classes lies within the pages of this book.

This chapter is devoted to helping you train your Hovawart at home. If the recommended procedures are followed faithfully, you may expect positive results that will prove rewarding both to you and your dog.

Whether your new charge is a puppy or a mature adult, the methods of teaching and the techniques we use in training basic behaviors are the same. After all, no dog, whether puppy or adult, likes harsh or inhumane methods. All creatures, however, respond favorably to gentle motivational methods and sincere praise and encouragement. Now let us get started.

HOUSE-TRAINING

You can train a puppy to relieve himself wherever you choose, but this must be somewhere suitable. You should bear in mind from the outset that when your puppy is old enough to go out in public places, any canine deposits must be removed at once. You will always have to carry with you a plastic bag or "poop-scoop."

Outdoor training includes

REAP THE REWARDS
If you start with a normal, healthy dog and give him time, patience and some carefully executed lessons, you will reap the rewards of that training for the life of the dog. And what a life it will be! The two of you will find immeasurable pleasure in the companionship you have built together with love, respect and understanding.

CANINE DEVELOPMENT SCHEDULE

It is important to understand how and at what age a puppy develops into adulthood. If you are a puppy owner, consult the following Canine Development Schedule to determine the stage of development your puppy is currently experiencing. This knowledge will help you as you work with the puppy in the weeks and months ahead.

Period	Age	Characteristics
First to Third	**Birth to Seven Weeks**	Puppy needs food, sleep and warmth, and responds to simple and gentle touching. Needs mother for security and disciplining. Needs littermates for learning and interacting with other dogs. Pup learns to function within a pack and learns pack order of dominance. Begin socializing pup with adults and children for short periods. Pup begins to become aware of his environment.
Fourth	**Eight to Twelve Weeks**	Brain is fully developed. Needs socializing with outside world. Remove from mother and littermates. Needs to change from canine pack to human pack. Human dominance necessary. Fear period occurs between 8 and 12 weeks. Avoid fright and pain.
Fifth	**Thirteen to Sixteen Weeks**	Training and formal obedience should begin. Less association with other dogs, more with people, places, situations. Period will pass easily if you remember this is pup's change-to-adolescence time. Be firm and fair. Flight instinct prominent. Permissiveness and over-disciplining can do permanent damage. Praise for good behavior.
Juvenile	**Four to Eight Months**	Another fear period about 7 to 8 months of age. It passes quickly, but be cautious of fright and pain. Sexual maturity reached. Dominant traits established. Dog should understand sit, down, come and stay by now.

NOTE: THESE ARE APPROXIMATE TIME FRAMES. ALLOW FOR INDIVIDUAL DIFFERENCES IN PUPPIES.

such surfaces as grass, soil and cement. Indoor training usually means training your dog to newspaper, although this is not usually a viable option for Hovawart owners, given the breed's size. When deciding on the surface and location that you will want your Hovawart to use, be sure it is going to be permanent. Training your dog to grass and then changing your mind a few months later is extremely difficult for both dog and owner.

Next, choose the command you will use each and every time you want your puppy to void. "Hurry up" and "Let's go" are examples of commands commonly used by dog owners. Get in the habit of giving the puppy your chosen relief command before you take him out. That way, when he becomes an adult, you will be able to determine if he wants to go out when you ask him. A confirmation will be signs of interest, such as

wagging his tail, watching you intently, going to the door, etc.

What a pleasure for all members of your family to share their lives with a well-trained Hovawart friend!

PUPPY'S NEEDS

Your puppy needs to relieve himself after play periods, after each meal, after he has been sleeping and at any time he indicates that he is looking for a place to urinate or defecate. The urinary and intestinal tract muscles of very young puppies are not fully developed. Therefore, like human babies, puppies need to relieve themselves frequently.

Take your puppy out often—every hour for an eight week old, for example—and always immediately after sleeping and eating. The older the puppy, the less often he will need to relieve himself. Finally, as a mature healthy adult, he will require only three to five relief trips per day.

CALM DOWN

Dogs will do anything for your attention. If you reward the dog when he is calm and attentive, you will develop a well-mannered dog. If, on the other hand, you greet your dog excitedly and encourage him to wrestle with you, the dog will greet you the same way and you will have a hyperactive dog on your hands.

HOUSING

Since the types of housing and control you provide for your puppy have a direct relationship on the success of house-training, we consider the various aspects of both before we begin training.

Taking a new puppy home and turning him loose in your house can be compared to turning a child loose in a sports arena and telling the child that the place is all his! The sheer enormity of the place would be too much for him to handle. Instead, offer the puppy clearly defined areas where he can play, sleep, eat and live. A room of the house where the family gathers is the most obvious choice. Puppies are social animals and need to feel a part of the pack right from the start. Hearing your voice, watching you while you are doing things and smelling you nearby are all positive reinforcers that he is now a member of your pack. Usually a family room, the kitchen or a nearby adjoining breakfast area is ideal for providing safety and security for both puppy and owner.

Within the designated room, there should be a smaller area that the puppy can call his own. An alcove, a wire or fiberglass dog crate or a gated (not boarded!) corner from which he can view the activities of his new family will be fine. The size of the area or crate is the key factor here. The area must be large enough so that

SAFETY FIRST

While it may seem that the most important things to your dog are eating, sleeping and chewing the upholstery on your furniture, his first concern is actually safety. The domesticated dogs we keep as companions have the same pack instinct as their ancestors who ran free thousands of years ago. Because of this pack instinct, your dog wants to know that he and his pack are not in danger of being harmed, and that his pack has a strong, capable leader. You must establish yourself as the leader early on in your relationship. That way your dog will trust that you will take care of him and the pack, and he will accept your commands without question.

the puppy can lie down and stretch out, as well as stand up, without rubbing his head on the top. At the same time, it must be small enough so that he cannot relieve himself at one end and sleep at the other without coming into contact with his droppings before he is fully trained to relieve himself outside. Dogs are, by nature, clean animals and will not remain close to their relief areas unless forced to do so. In those cases, they then become dirty dogs and usually remain that way for life.

The dog's designated area should contain clean bedding and

a toy. Do not put food or water in the dog's crate or area until house-training has been accomplished reliably, as eating and drinking stimulate the dog's digestive processes and will defeat your training purposes! Once trained, water should always be available, in a non-spill container.

CONTROL

By *control*, we mean helping the puppy to create a lifestyle pattern that will be compatible to that of his human pack (*you*!). Just as we guide little children to learn our way of life, we must show the puppy when it is time to play, eat, sleep, exercise and even entertain himself.

Your puppy should always sleep in his crate. He should also learn that, during times of house-hold confusion and excessive human activity, such as at break-fast when family members are preparing for the day, he can play

by himself in relative safety and comfort in his designated area. Each time you leave the puppy alone, he should understand exactly where he is to stay.

Puppies are chewers and cannot tell the difference between things like lamp and television wires, shoes, table legs, etc. Chewing into a television wire, for example, can be fatal to the puppy, while a shorted wire can start a fire in the house. If the puppy chews on the arm of the chair when he is alone, you will probably discipline him angrily when you get home. Thus, he makes the association that your coming home means he is going to be punished. (He will not remem-ber chewing the chair and is inca-pable of making the association of the discipline with his naughty

Crate training is the method of choice around the world for teaching dogs clean and safe living habits.

HIS OWN LITTLE CORNER

Mealtime should be a peaceful time for your puppy. Do not put his food and water bowls in a high-traffic area in the house. For example, give him his own little corner of the kitchen where he can eat undisturbed and where he will not be underfoot. Do not allow small children or other family members to disturb the pup when he is eating.

deed.) Accustoming the pup to his designated area not only keeps him safe but also avoids his engaging in destructive behaviors when you are not around.

Times of excitement, such as special occasions, family parties, etc., can be fun for the puppy, providing that he can view the activities from the security of his designated area. He is not underfoot and he is not being fed all sorts of tidbits that will probably cause him stomach distress, yet he still feels a part of the fun.

SCHEDULE
A puppy should be taken to his relief area each time he is released from his designated area, after

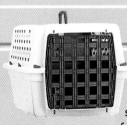

THE SUCCESS METHOD

Success that comes by luck is usually short-lived. Success that comes by well-thought-out proven methods is often more easily achieved and permanent. This is the Success Method. It is designed to give you, the puppy owner, a simple yet proven way to help your puppy develop clean living habits and a feeling of security in his new environment.

6 Steps to Successful Crate Training

1 Tell the puppy "Crate time!" and place him in the crate with a small treat (a piece of cheese or half of a biscuit). Let him stay in the crate for five minutes while you are in the same room. Then release him and praise lavishly. Never release him when he is fussing. Wait until he is quiet before you let him out.

2 Repeat Step 1 several times a day.

3 The next day, place the puppy in the crate as before. Let him stay there for ten minutes. Do this several times.

4 Continue building time in five-minute increments until the puppy stays in his crate for 30 minutes with you in the room. Always take him to his relief area after prolonged periods in his crate.

5 Now go back to Step 1 and let the puppy stay in his crate for five minutes, this time while you are out of the room.

6 Once again, build crate time in five-minute increments with you out of the room. When the puppy will stay willingly in his crate (he may even fall asleep!) for 30 minutes with you out of the room, he will be ready to stay in it for several hours at a time.

meals, after play sessions and when he first awakens in the morning (at age eight weeks, this can mean 5 a.m.!). The puppy will indicate that he's ready "to go" by circling or sniffing busily—do not misinterpret these signs. For a puppy less than ten weeks of age, a routine of taking him out every hour is necessary. As the puppy grows, he will be able to wait for longer periods of time.

Keep trips to his relief area short. Stay no more than five or six minutes and then return to the house. If he goes during that time, praise him lavishly and take him indoors immediately. If he does not, but he has an accident when you go back indoors, pick him up immediately, say "No! No!" and return to his relief area. Wait a few minutes, then return to the house again. Never hit a puppy or put his face in urine or excrement when he has had an accident!

Once indoors, put the puppy in his crate until you have had time to clean up his accident. Then, release him to the family area and watch him more closely than before. Chances are, his accident was a result of your not picking up his signal or waiting too long before offering him the opportunity to relieve himself. Never hold a grudge against the puppy for accidents.

Let the puppy learn that going outdoors means it is time to relieve himself, not to play. Once

Always clean up after your dog, whether you're in a public place or your own yard.

trained, he will be able to play indoors and out and still differentiate between the times for play versus the times for relief. Help him develop regular hours for naps, being alone, playing by himself and just resting, all in his crate. Encourage him to entertain himself while you are busy with your activities. Let him learn that having you near is comforting, but it is not your main purpose in life to provide him with your undivided attention. Each time you put your puppy in his own area,

HOW MANY TIMES A DAY?

AGE	RELIEF TRIPS
To 14 weeks	10
14–22 weeks	8
22–32 weeks	6
Adulthood	4
(dog stops growing)	

These are estimates, of course, but they are a guide to the *minimum* number of opportunities a dog should have each day to relieve himself.

Accustoming your pup to his collar and lead is necessary for house-training purposes, teaching basic commands, taking regular walks and general good behavior.

use the same command, whatever suits best. Soon he will run to his crate or special area when he hears you say those words.

Crate training provides safety for you, the puppy and the home. It also provides the puppy with a feeling of security, and that helps the puppy achieve self-confidence and clean habits. Remember that one of the primary ingredients in house-training your puppy is control. Regardless of your lifestyle, there will always be occasions when you will need to have a place where your dog can stay and be happy and safe. Crate training is the answer for now and in the future.

In conclusion, a few key elements are really all you need for a successful house-training method—consistency, frequency,

praise, control and supervision. By following these procedures with a normal, healthy puppy, you and the puppy will soon be past the stage of "accidents" and ready to move on to a full and rewarding life together.

ROLES OF DISCIPLINE, REWARD AND PUNISHMENT

Discipline, training one to act in accordance with rules, brings order to life. It is as simple as that. Without discipline, particularly in a group society, chaos will reign supreme and the group will eventually perish. Humans and canines are social animals and need some form of discipline in order to function effectively. They must procure food, reproduce to keep their species going and protect their home base and their young. If there were no discipline in the lives of social animals, they would eventually die from starvation and/or predation by other stronger animals. In the case of domestic canines, discipline in their lives is needed in order for them to understand how their pack (you and other family members) functions and how they must act in order to survive.

A large humane society in a

DON'T GO TO BED MAD!
A dog should never go to bed under punishment, just like it's advised for humans never to go to bed angry!

highly populated area recently surveyed dog owners regarding their satisfaction with their relationships with their dogs. People who had trained their dogs were 75% more satisfied with their pets than those who had never trained their dogs.

Dr. Edward Thorndike, a noted psychologist, established *Thorndike's Theory of Learning*, which states that a behavior that results in a pleasant event tends to be repeated. Furthermore, it concludes that a behavior that results in an unpleasant event tends not to be repeated. It is this theory upon which training methods are based today. For example, if you manipulate a dog to perform a specific behavior and reward him for doing it, he is likely to do it again because he enjoyed the end result.

Occasionally, punishment, a penalty inflicted for an offense, is necessary. The best type of punishment often comes from an outside source. For example, a child is told not to touch the stove because he may get burned. He disobeys and touches the stove. In doing so, he receives a burn. From that time on, he respects the heat of the stove and avoids contact with it. Therefore, a behavior that results in an unpleasant event tends not to be repeated.

A good example of a dog's learning the hard way is the dog who chases the house cat. He is

LANGUAGE BARRIER

Dogs do not understand our language and have to rely on tone of voice more than just words or sound. They can be trained to react to a certain sound, at a certain volume. If you say "No, Oliver" in a very soft, pleasant voice, it will not have the same meaning as "No, Oliver!!" when you raise your voice. You should never use the dog's name during a reprimand, just the command "No! " You never want the dog to associate his name with a negative experience or reprimand.

Produce a treat and watch your Hovawart snap to attention!

able to work, not too heavy for the dog and perfectly safe.

TREATS

Have a bag of treats on hand; something nutritious and easy to swallow works best. Use a soft treat, a chunk of cheese or a piece of cooked chicken rather than a dry biscuit. By the time the dog has finished chewing a dry treat, he will forget why he is being rewarded in the first place!

Using food rewards will not teach a dog to beg at the table—the only way to teach a dog to beg at the table is to give him food from the table. In training, rewarding the dog with a food treat will help him associate praise and the treats with learning new behaviors that obviously please his owner.

told many times to leave the cat alone, yet he persists in teasing the cat. Then, one day, the dog begins chasing the cat but the cat turns and swipes a claw across the dog's face, leaving the dog with a painful gash on his nose. The final result is that the dog stops chasing the cat.

TRAINING EQUIPMENT

COLLAR AND LEAD

For a Hovawart, the collar and lead that you use for training must be one with which you are easily

TRAINING BEGINS: ASK THE DOG A QUESTION

In order to teach your dog anything, you must first get his attention. After all, he cannot learn anything if he is looking away from you with his mind on something else.

To get your dog's attention, ask him "School?" and immediately walk over to him and give him a treat as you tell him "Good dog." Wait a minute or two and repeat the routine, this time with a treat in your hand as you approach within a foot of the dog. Do not go directly to him, but stop

about a foot short of him and hold
out the treat as you ask "School?"
He will see you approaching with
a treat in your hand and most
likely begin walking toward you.
As you meet, give him the treat
and praise again.

The third time, ask the question, have a treat in your hand
and walk only a short distance
toward the dog so that he must
walk almost all the way to you.
As he reaches you, give him the
treat and praise again.

By this time, the dog will
probably be getting the idea that if
he pays attention to you, especially when you ask that question,
it will pay off in treats and enjoyable activities for him. In other
words, he learns that "school"
means doing great things with you
that are fun and that result in
positive attention for him.

Remember that the dog does
not understand your verbal
language; he only recognizes
sounds. Your question translates
to a series of sounds for him, and
those sounds become the signal to
go to you and pay attention. The
dog learns that if he does this, he
will get to interact with you plus
receive treats and praise.

THE BASIC COMMANDS
The education of your Hovawart
will involve the essential
commands: sit, down, heel, come,
etc., all of which should be given
briefly and rapidly, first using the
dog's name to ensure his attention. These basics are very important for the education and training
of your friend. The commands
should be given firmly, without
pressure. Every satisfactory
response should be rewarded with
praise and perhaps a treat.

The basic commands are
taught very early in the dog's life.
If you and your Hovawart attend
obedience classes, you will be
taught the simple techniques to
ensure that your dog obeys. The
Hovawart needs commands to be

The head goes up,
the bottom goes
down...teaching
the sit is based on
a very simple
principle.

repeated without anger or frustration. Training sessions should be kept short and fun, and once you have completed a training session, give the dog his freedom with a "Go!" or "OK!" and play with him for a few minutes. Once you've succeeded in the basic commands, you can graduate to more difficult exercises such as "Fetch," always being sure to exhibit patience and rewarding the dog with plenty of praise and encouragement.

TEACHING SIT

Once you have the dog's attention, attach his lead and hold it in your left hand, and hold a food treat in your right hand. Place your food hand at the dog's nose and let him lick the treat but not take it from you. Say "Sit" and slowly raise your food hand from in front of the dog's nose up over his head so that he is looking at the ceiling. As he bends his head upward, he will have to bend his knees to maintain his balance. As he bends

his knees, he will assume a sit position. At that point, release the food treat and praise lavishly with comments such as "Good dog! Good sit!," etc. Remember to always praise enthusiastically, because dogs relish verbal praise from their owners and feel so proud of themselves whenever they accomplish a behavior.

You will not use food forever in getting the dog to obey your commands. Food is only used to teach new behaviors and, once the dog knows what you want when you give a specific command, you will wean him off the food treats but still maintain the verbal praise. After all, you will always have your voice with you, and there will be many times when you have no food rewards but expect the dog to obey.

TEACHING DOWN

Teaching the down exercise is easy when you understand how the dog perceives the down position, and it is very difficult when you do not. Dogs perceive the down position as a submissive one; therefore, teaching the down exercise by using a forceful method can sometimes make the dog develop such a fear of the down that he either runs away when you say "Down" or he attempts to snap at the person who tries to force him down.

Have the dog sit close alongside your left leg, facing in the

THE GOLDEN RULE

The golden rule of dog training is simple. For each "question" (command), there is only one correct answer (reaction). One command = one reaction. Keep practicing the command until the dog reacts correctly without hesitating. Be repetitive but not monotonous. Dogs get bored just as people do!

From the sit, you can progress to the down, which may require a little more patience on your part, but should not be too difficult to teach.

same direction as you are. Hold the lead in your left hand and a food treat in your right. Now place your left hand lightly on the top of the dog's shoulders where they meet above the spinal cord. Do not push down on the dog's shoulders; simply rest your left hand there so you can guide the dog to lie down close to your left leg rather than to swing away from your side when he drops.

Now place the food hand at the dog's nose, say "Down" very softly (almost a whisper) and

slowly lower the food hand to the dog's front feet. When the food hand reaches the floor, begin moving it forward along the floor in front of the dog. Keep talking softly to the dog, saying things like, "Do you want this treat? You can do this, good dog." Your reassuring tone of voice will help calm the dog as he tries to follow the food hand in order to get the treat.

When the dog's elbows touch the floor, release the food and praise softly. Try to get the dog to maintain that down position for several seconds before you let him sit up again. The goal here is to get the dog to settle down and not feel threatened in the down position.

TEACHING STAY

It is easy to teach the dog to stay in either a sit or a down position. Again, we use food and praise during the teaching process as we help the dog to understand exactly what it is that we are expecting him to do.

To teach the sit/stay, start with the dog sitting on your left side as before and hold the lead in your left hand. Have a food treat in your right hand and place your food hand at the dog's nose. Say "Stay" and step out on your right foot to stand directly in front of the dog, toe to toe, as he licks and nibbles the treat. Be sure to keep his head facing upward to main-

DOUBLE JEOPARDY

A dog in jeopardy never lies down. He stays alert on his feet because instinct tells him that he may have to run away or fight for his survival. Therefore, if a dog feels threatened or anxious, he will not lie down. Consequently, it is important to keep the dog calm and relaxed as he learns the down exercise.

tain the sit position. Count to five and then swing around to stand next to the dog again with him on your left. As soon as you get back to the original position, release the food and praise lavishly.

To teach the down/stay, do the down as previously described. As soon as the dog lies down, say "Stay" and step out on your right foot just as you did in the sit/stay. Count to five and then return to stand beside the dog with him on your left side. Release the treat and praise as always.

Within a week or ten days, you can begin to add a bit of distance between you and your dog when you leave him. When you do, use your left hand open with the palm facing the dog as a stay signal, much the same as the hand signal a police officer uses to stop traffic at an intersection. Hold the food treat in your right hand as before, but this time the food will not be touching the dog's nose. He will watch the food hand and quickly learn that he is going to get that treat as soon as you return to his side.

When you can stand 3 feet away from your dog for 30 seconds, you can then begin building time and distance in both stays. Eventually, the dog can be expected to remain in the stay position for prolonged periods of time until you return to him or call him to you. Always praise lavishly when he stays.

CONSISTENCY PAYS OFF

Dogs need consistency in their feeding schedule, exercise and relief visits, and in the verbal commands you use. If you use "Stay" on Monday and "Stay here, please" on Tuesday, you will confuse your dog. Don't demand perfect behavior during training sessions and then let him have the run of the house the rest of the day. Above all, lavish praise on your pet consistently every time he does something right. The more he feels he is pleasing you, the more willing he will be to learn.

TEACHING COME

If you make teaching "come" an exciting experience, you should never have a "student" that does not love the game or that fails to come when called. The secret, it seems, is never to teach the word "come."

him and to get a treat as a reward for "winning."

A few turns of the "Where are you?" game and the dog will understand that everyone is playing the game and that each person has a big celebration awaiting the dog's success at locating him or her. Once the dog learns to love the game, simply calling out "Where are you?" will bring him running from wherever he is when he hears that all-important question. You can also practice this command with the dog on a long lead. Call him to you, and greet his arrival with a treat and lots of praise.

The come command is recognized as one of the most important things to teach a dog, but there are trainers who work with thousands of dogs and never use the actual word "come." Yet these dogs will race to respond to a person who uses the dog's name followed by "Where are you?" For example, a woman has a 12-year-old companion dog who went

At times when an owner most wants his dog to come when called, the owner is likely to be upset or anxious and he allows these feelings to come through in the tone of his voice when he calls his dog. Hearing that desperation in his owner's voice, the dog fears the results of going to him and therefore either disobeys outright or runs in the opposite direction. The secret, therefore, is to teach the dog a game and, when you want him to come to you, simply play the game. It is practically a no-fail solution!

To begin, have several members of your family take a few food treats and each go into a different room in the house. Everyone takes turns calling the dog, and each person should celebrate the dog's finding him with a treat and lots of happy praise. When a person calls the dog, he is actually inviting the dog to find

> ### "COME" . . . BACK
> Never call your dog to come to you for a correction or scold him when he reaches you. That is the quickest way to turn a come command into "Go away fast!" Dogs think only in the present tense, and your dog will connect the scolding with coming to you, not with the misbehavior of a few moments earlier.

blind, but who never fails to
locate her owner when asked
"Where are you?"

Children, in particular, love to
play this game with their dogs.
Children can hide in smaller
places like a shower or bathtub,
behind a bed or under a table. The
dog needs to work a little bit
harder to find these hiding places,
but, when he does, he loves to
celebrate with a treat and a tussle
with a favorite youngster.

TEACHING HEEL

Heeling means that the dog walks
beside the owner without pulling.
It takes time and patience on the
owner's part to succeed at teaching the dog that he (the owner)

will not proceed unless the dog is
walking calmly beside him.
Neither pulling out ahead on the
lead nor lagging behind is
acceptable.

Begin by holding the lead in
your left hand as the dog sits
beside your left leg. Move the
loop end of the lead to your right
hand, but keep your left hand
short on the lead so that it keeps
the dog in close next to you.

Say "Heel" and step forward
on your left foot. Keep the dog
close to you and take three steps.
Stop and have the dog sit next to
you in what we now call the heel
position. Praise verbally, but do

Time for a walk!
Walking your
Hovawart daily is
great exercise for
dog and owner,
and a wonderful
opportunity to
spend time
together.

Heeling is a necessary command for all dogs, but show dogs will have to demonstrate the heel in the show ring as the judge evaluates their movement.

exercise is finished and the dog is free to relax.

If you are dealing with a dog who insists on pulling you around, simply "put on your brakes" and stand your ground so that the dog realizes that the two of you are not going anywhere until he is beside you and moving at your pace, not his. It may take some time just standing there to convince the dog that you are the leader and that you will be the one to decide on the direction and speed of your travel.

Each time the dog looks up at you or slows down to give a slack lead between the two of you, quietly praise him and say, "Good heel. Good dog." Eventually, the dog will begin to respond and within a few days he will be walking politely beside you without pulling on the lead. At first, the training sessions should be kept short and very positive; soon the dog will be able to walk nicely with you for increasingly longer distances. Remember also to give the dog free time and the opportu-

not touch the dog. Hesitate a moment and begin again with "Heel," taking three steps and stopping, at which point the dog is told to sit again.

Your goal here is to have the dog walk those three steps without pulling on the lead. Once he will walk calmly beside you for three steps without pulling, increase the number of steps you take to five. When he will walk politely beside you while you take five steps, you can increase the length of your walk to ten steps. Keep increasing the length of your stroll until the dog will walk quietly beside you without pulling as long as you want him to heel. When you stop heeling, indicate to the dog that the exercise is over by verbally praising as you pet him and say "OK, good dog." The "OK" is used as a release word, meaning that the

HEELING WELL

Teach your dog to heel in an enclosed area. Once you think that the dog will obey reliably and you want to attempt advanced obedience exercises such as off-lead heeling, test him in a fenced-in area so he cannot run away.

nity to run and play when you have finished heel practice.

WEANING OFF FOOD IN TRAINING

Food is used in training new behaviors. Once the dog understands what behavior goes with a specific command, it is time to start weaning him off the food treats. At first, give a treat after each exercise. Then, start to give a treat only after every other exercise. Mix up the times when you offer a food reward and the times when you only offer praise so that the dog will never know when he is going to receive both food and praise and when he is going to receive only praise. This is called a variable ratio reward system. It proves successful because there is always the chance that the owner will produce a treat, so the dog never stops trying for that reward. No matter what, *always* give verbal praise.

OBEDIENCE CLASSES

It is a good idea to enroll in an obedience class if one is available in your area. If yours is a show dog, showing classes would be more appropriate to prepare both of you for the ring. Many areas have dog clubs that offer basic obedience training as well as preparatory classes for obedience competition. There are also local dog trainers who offer similar classes.

At obedience trials, dogs can earn titles at various levels of competition. The beginning levels of obedience competition include basic behaviors such as sit, down, heel, etc. The more advanced levels of competition include jumping, retrieving, scent discrimination and signal work. The advanced levels require a dog and owner to put a lot of time and effort into their training, and training for obedience is best done in a relaxed, playful atmosphere without any air of constraint. Obedience is a discipline that requires a great deal of precision in the execution of the different exercises, which increase in difficulty according to class. The titles that can be earned at these levels of competition are very prestigious. Obedience is an excellent

Training for an advanced obedience exercise, retrieving the dumbbell.

discipline, for it serves as a stage to test other possibilities for your Hovawart.

TRAINING FOR OTHER ACTIVITIES

There are many activities that you can share with your Hovawart once you've succeeded with the basic commands and you know that your dog will respond reliably. For example, teaching the dog to help out around the home, in the garden or on the farm provides great satisfaction to both dog and owner. In addition, the dog's help makes life a little easier for his owner and raises his stature as a valued companion to his family. It helps give the dog a purpose by occupying his mind and providing an outlet for his energy.

Backpacking is an exciting and healthy activity that the dog can be taught without assistance from more than his owner. The

The long stay is another exercise in advanced obedience competition.

THE VERSATILE HOVAWART

The sampling of activities discussed here shows that your Hovawart has enormous potential. It is up to you to decide how to develop this potential. Did you know:

- That a Derrick survey was performed by a Hovawart?
- That more and more Hovawarts are being used as guide dogs for the sight-impaired?
- That in Nordic countries the Hovawart has been used as a *chien de trait* to deliver mail?
- That the Hovawart is used for its sense of smell by customs authorities?
- That there are Hovawart bike competitions?

---

exercise of walking and climbing is good for man and dog alike, and the bond that they develop together is priceless. The rule for backpacking with any dog is never to expect the dog to carry more than one-sixth of his body weight.

WORK

The notion of work in a dog consists of using the qualities that exist in a specific breed and improving upon them. As we have noted, the Hovawart is an excellent watchdog, protecting his human family and their property. Certain disciplines can help the

In an obedience class, dogs and handlers learn together, providing opportunities for both education and socialization.

Hovawart reach his potential in such work. Maria Kuncewicz gives us a brief summary: "The Hovawart is an excellent multi-purpose work dog. You can try out a number of tasks with your companion and the dog will prove to be very good at a few of them. You need to know how to motivate the animal using different methods, being careful how firm you become because the Hovawart is a sensitive and intelligent dog that also knows how to be stubborn. Avoid too much repetition so as not to tire the dog. Increase the level of difficulty of a given task to keep its interest."

TRACKING

Without doubt, the Hovawart is naturally adept at tracking because it usually gives the dog complete freedom of movement. Following are some specialized types of tracking trials that you may wish to undertake with your Hovawart.

Practical Search: This is a fairly new discipline, which tests the dog's scenting abilities. The aim is for the dog to find a person (or people) that are hiding. The trials are carried out at three

THE RING

Very typically French, the Ring demands exceptional physical performances of a dog: obedience, jumping and biting. Due to the efforts required in both long and high jumps, this discipline is better suited for German Shepherds. Mondioring is similar to the Ring, but is carried out in a more realistic setting, which leaves more scope for initiative. It is growing more popular internationally.

In the Practical Search, Loula, a female Hovawart, first works to pick up and follow the scent.

levels: 1, 2 and Certificate. The first two levels are carried out over a distance of 2 kilometers, the Certificate level at 3 kilometers.

Level 1 takes place in the countryside, where the person to be found leaves an object in the departure zone (1200 square

OTHER DISCIPLINES

Other disciplines are also suitable for the Hovawart:

• Practical work in the countryside: Similar to the Ring trials, but with an expanded area of action. Tests are carried out on different types of terrain with natural obstacles.
• "Cavage": Searching for truffles buried the day before in different types of terrain. This test is timed.
• Canicross: A race course that involves things like long-distance running, biking and sleighing. As with agility trials, the dog should be full grown before training for and taking part in this discipline.
• Guide for the sight-impaired: This type of assistance work requires courage and flexibility, which fits the Hovawart's character very well.

The Hovawart follows her nose up and over a wall.

meters) to attract and motivate the dog. The dog and his handler leave two hours after the scent is laid by the person, and they have one hour to find where the person is hiding. Level 2 includes a built-up urban area and a larger departure zone (2500 square meters). The dog and handler leave three hours after the target person, whom they have one-and-a-half hours to find. The Certificate level involves a departure zone of 5000 square meters with two people laying the scent, and a six-hour interval before the dog and handler are allowed to track them, which they must do in two hours.

French Tracking: In this discipline, two stakes placed in the ground 10 meters apart lay the scent. Unlike the Practical Search method, the dog is allowed to pick up the scent immediately. This trial has two distinct tests: the "open" track, in which the dog must retrieve objects, and a course that the dog must complete without a handler.

The "A" and "B" trials (open track) are rewarded with a certificate. The "C" trial, in which the dog is alone, is very difficult as the scent is cut by two false trails. The "bloodhound feature" trail, which is part of the highest level, involves the dog's identifying a tracker while followed by his handler with the help of a tether. The Hovawart is required to find three objects, follow a trail (of some 1000 paces), which branches off seven times, and cross three false trails until he is able to identify the target person out of a group of three people.

FCI Tracking: This discipline involves a trail of about 2000 paces with seven twists and seven objects to find. The scent is placed three hours prior to the trial and includes two false trails prepared half an hour before the dog departs. The dog is on a tether that does not allow him to stray more than 10 meters in any direction. This very rigorous trial begins in a 20 x 20-meter zone, in

which lies an object that indicates to the dog the direction in which to begin.

AGILITY

In spite of its size, the Hovawart is supple and agile. If you are an active person and own a cheerful dog, then this area of the dog sport is for you. The course is composed of different obstacles (hurdles, tunnels, jumps, passages, etc.) to be covered as quickly and accurately as possi-

Success! Loula has found the person!

ble. Remember that your Hovawart is a Molosser and that training for agility should not begin too early. Most recommend waiting until your dog is at least 12 months of age to begin agility training, and dogs under one year old are not eligible to compete.

THE RCI

This discipline, which usually features the German Schutzund, is well suited to Hovawarts as there are no long periods of work repetition; rather, it offers diversity through tests of tracking, obedience and defense biting. Based on international selection, the RCI trials are simpler than the aforementioned types of tracking trials.

Schutzhund originated as a test to determine the best-quality dogs to be used for breeding stock. Breeders continue to use it as a way to evaluate working ability and temperament. There are three levels in Schutzhund trials, and each level consists of training, obedience and protection phases. Training for Schutzhund is intense and must be practiced consistently to keep the dog keen. The experience of RCI and Schutzhund training is very rewarding for dog and owner, and the Hovawart's tractability is well suited for this type of training.

Through the tire jump, one of the obstacles in an agility trial.

Sleeve training is part of Schutzhund defense work.

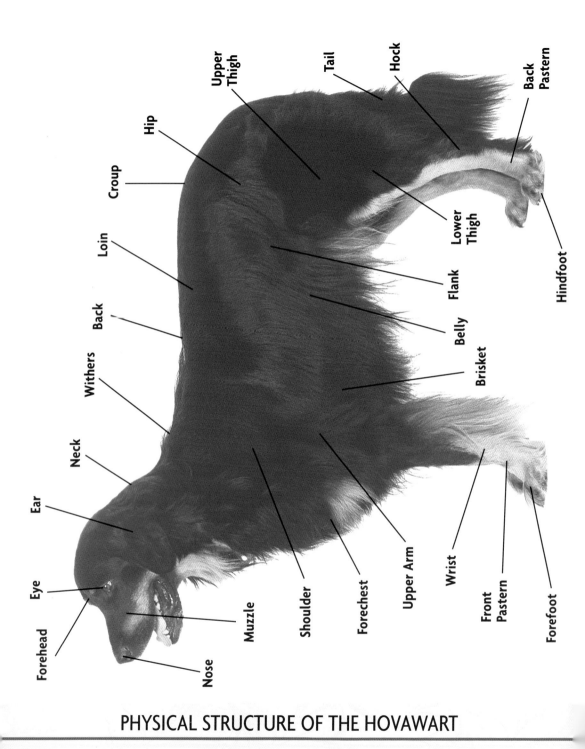

PHYSICAL STRUCTURE OF THE HOVAWART

Upper Thigh

Tail

Hock

Back Pastern

Hip

Croup

Lower Thigh

Loin

Flank

Back

Belly

Hindfoot

Withers

Brisket

Neck

Ear

Eye

Forehead

Nose

Muzzle

Shoulder

Forechest

Upper Arm

Wrist

Front Pastern

Forefoot

Dogs suffer from many of the same physical illnesses as people and might even share many of the same psychological problems. Since people usually know more about human diseases than canine maladies, many of the terms used in this chapter will be familiar but not necessarily those used by vets. For example, we will use the familiar term *x-ray* instead of *radiograph*. We will also use the familiar term *symptoms*, even though dogs don't have symptoms, which are verbal descriptions of something the patient feels or observes himself that he regards as abnormal. Dogs have *clinical signs* since they cannot speak, so we have to look for these clinical signs...but we still use the term *symptoms* in the book.

Medicine is a constantly changing art, with of course scientific input as well. Things alter as we learn more and more about basic sciences such as genetics and biochemistry, and have use of more sophisticated imaging techniques like Computer Aided Tomography (CAT scans) or Magnetic Resonance Imaging (MRI scans). There is academic dispute about many canine maladies, so different vets may treat them in different ways. For example, some vets place a greater emphasis on surgical treatment than others.

SELECTING A VET

Your selection of a vet should be based on personal recommendation for his skills with small animals, especially dogs. If the vet is based nearby, it will be helpful because you might have an emergency or need to make multiple visits for treatments.

All vets are licensed and should be capable of dealing with routine medical issues such as infections, injuries and the promotion of health (for example, by vaccination). If the problem affecting your dog is more complex, your vet will refer your pet to someone with a more detailed knowledge of what is wrong. This will usually be a specialist who concentrates in a certain field, e.g., veterinary dermatology, veterinary ophthalmology, etc.; whatever is relevant to your dog's problem.

Veterinary procedures are very costly and, as the treatments

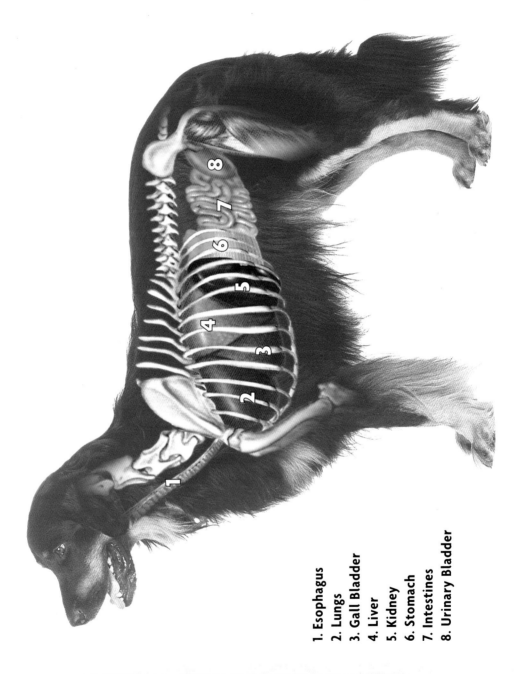

1. Esophagus
2. Lungs
3. Gall Bladder
4. Liver
5. Kidney
6. Stomach
7. Intestines
8. Urinary Bladder

INTERNAL ORGANS OF THE HOVAWART

available improve, they become more expensive. It is quite acceptable to discuss matters of cost with your vet; if there is more than one treatment option, cost may be a factor in deciding which route to take.

Insurance against veterinary cost is also becoming very popular. Policies can range from those covering the costs of diseases and unexpected emergencies to those that cover your dog's routine health care.

Breakdown of Veterinary Income by Category

2%	Dentistry
4%	Radiology
12%	Surgery
15%	Vaccinations
19%	Laboratory
23%	Examinations
25%	Medicines

PREVENTATIVE MEDICINE

It is much easier, less costly and more effective to practice preventative medicine than to fight bouts of illness and disease. Properly

A SKUNKY PROBLEM

Have you noticed your dog dragging his rump along the floor? If so, it is likely that his anal sacs are impacted or possibly infected. The anal sacs are small pouches located on both sides of the anus under the skin and muscles. They are about the size and shape of a grape and contain a foul-smelling liquid. Their contents are usually emptied when the dog has a bowel movement but, if not emptied completely, they will impact, which will cause your dog much pain. Fortunately, your veterinarian can tend to this problem easily by draining the sacs for the dog. Be aware that your dog might also empty his anal sacs in cases of extreme fright.

bred puppies of all breeds come from parents that were selected based upon their genetic-disease profiles. The puppies' dam should have been vaccinated, free of all internal and external parasites and properly nourished. For these reasons, a visit to the vet who cared for the dam is recommended if at all possible. The dam passes disease resistance to her puppies, which should last from eight to ten weeks. Unfortunately, she can also pass on parasites and infection. This is why knowledge about her health is useful in learning more about the health of the puppies.

WEANING TO FIVE MONTHS OLD

Puppies should be weaned by the time they are two months old. A puppy that remains for at least eight weeks with his dam and littermates usually adapts better

A typical vet's income, categorized according to services performed. This survey dealt with small-animal (pets) practices.

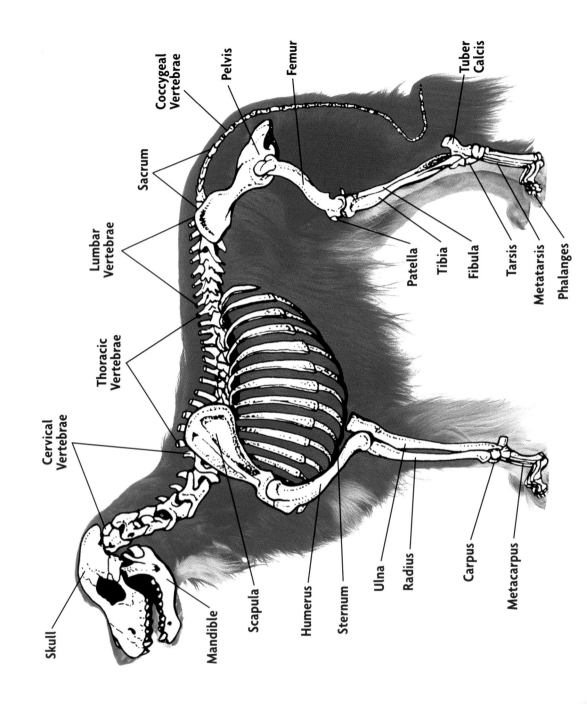

Coccygeal Vertebrae

Pelvis

Femur

Tuber Calcis

Sacrum

Tibia

Fibula

Tarsis

Metatarsis

Phalanges

Patella

Lumbar Vertebrae

Thoracic Vertebrae

Cervical Vertebrae

Skull

Mandible

Scapula

Humerus

Sternum

Ulna

Radius

Carpus

Metacarpus

SKELETAL STRUCTURE OF THE HOVAWART

to other dogs and people later in his life.

Sometimes new owners have their puppy examined by a vet immediately, which is a good idea unless the puppy is overtired by a long journey. In that case, a visit within the next day or so is very important to ensure that the pup does not have any problems that are not apparent.

The puppy will have his teeth examined and his skeletal conformation and general health checked prior to certification by the vet. Puppies in certain breeds have problems with their kneecaps, cataracts and other eye problems, heart murmurs and undescended testicles. They may also have personality problems and your vet might have training in temperament testing and evaluation. Also at the first visit, your vet will set up a schedule for the pup's vaccinations.

VACCINATIONS

Most vaccinations are given by injection and should only be given by a vet. Both he and you should keep a record of the date of the injection, the identification of the vaccine and the amount

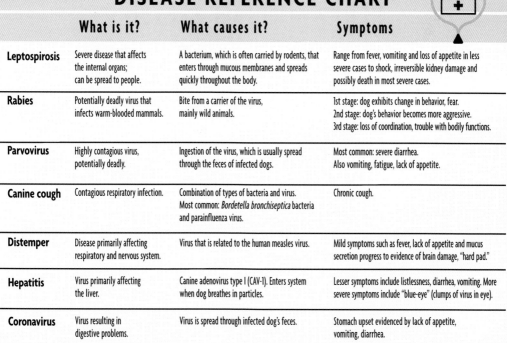

DISEASE REFERENCE CHART

	What is it?	What causes it?	Symptoms
Leptospirosis	Severe disease that affects the internal organs; can be spread to people.	A bacterium, which is often carried by rodents, that enters through mucous membranes and spreads quickly throughout the body.	Range from fever, vomiting and loss of appetite in less severe cases to shock, irreversible kidney damage and possibly death in most severe cases.
Rabies	Potentially deadly virus that infects warm-blooded mammals.	Bite from a carrier of the virus, mainly wild animals.	1st stage: dog exhibits change in behavior, fear. 2nd stage: dog's behavior becomes more aggressive. 3rd stage: loss of coordination, trouble with bodily functions.
Parvovirus	Highly contagious virus, potentially deadly.	Ingestion of the virus, which is usually spread through the feces of infected dogs.	Most common: severe diarrhea. Also vomiting, fatigue, lack of appetite.
Canine cough	Contagious respiratory infection.	Combination of types of bacteria and virus. Most common: *Bordetella bronchiseptica* bacteria and parainfluenza virus.	Chronic cough.
Distemper	Disease primarily affecting respiratory and nervous system.	Virus that is related to the human measles virus.	Mild symptoms such as fever, lack of appetite and mucus secretion progress to evidence of brain damage, "hard pad."
Hepatitis	Virus primarily affecting the liver.	Canine adenovirus type I (CAV-1). Enters system when dog breathes in particles.	Lesser symptoms include listlessness, diarrhea, vomiting. More severe symptoms include "blue-eye" (clumps of virus in eye).
Coronavirus	Virus resulting in digestive problems.	Virus is spread through infected dog's feces.	Stomach upset evidenced by lack of appetite, vomiting, diarrhea.

To administer a pill to your Hovawart, first place the pill at the back of the dog's mouth.

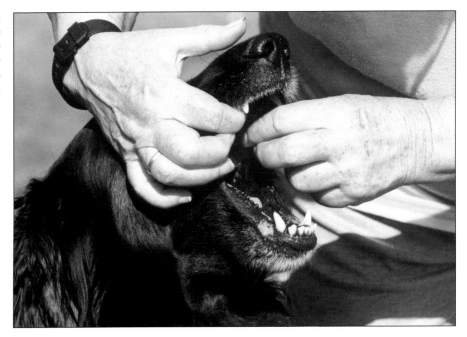

Stroke his throat to encourage him to swallow. Once he's swallowed, check his mouth to make sure that the pill went down.

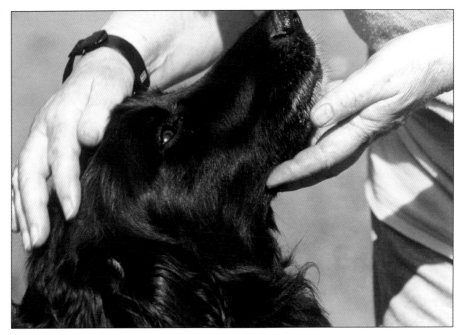

given. Some vets give a first vaccination at eight weeks, but most dog breeders prefer the course not to commence until about ten weeks because of the risk of interaction with the antibodies produced by the mother. The vaccination schedule is usually based on a 15-day cycle. You must take your vet's advice as to when to vaccinate, as this may differ according to the vaccine used.

The usual vaccines contain immunizing doses of several different viruses such as distemper, parvovirus, parainfluenza and hepatitis. There are other vaccines available when the puppy is at risk. You should always rely upon professional advice. This is especially true for the booster immunizations. Most vaccination programs require a booster when the puppy is a year old and once a year thereafter. In some cases, circumstances may require more or less frequent immunizations.

Kennel or canine cough, more formally known as tracheobronchitis, is immunized against with a vaccine that is sprayed into the dog's nostrils. Canine cough is usually included in routine vacci-

HEALTH AND VACCINATION SCHEDULE

AGE IN WEEKS:	6TH	8TH	10TH	12TH	14TH	16TH	20-24TH	52ND
Worm Control	✔	✔	✔	✔	✔	✔	✔	
Neutering								✔
Heartworm		✔		✔		✔	✔	
Parvovirus	✔		✔		✔		✔	✔
Distemper		✔		✔		✔		✔
Hepatitis		✔		✔		✔		✔
Leptospirosis								✔
Parainfluenza	✔		✔		✔			✔
Dental Examination		✔					✔	✔
Complete Physical		✔					✔	✔
Coronavirus					✔		✔	✔
Canine Cough	✔							
Hip Dysplasia								✔
Rabies							✔	

Vaccinations are not instantly effective. It takes about two weeks for the dog's immune system to develop antibodies. Most vaccinations require annual booster shots. Your vet should guide you in this regard.

nation, but it is often not as effective as the vaccines for other major diseases.

FIVE MONTHS TO ONE YEAR OF AGE
Unless you intend to breed or show your dog, neutering the puppy around six months of age is recommended. Discuss this with your vet, as opinions vary regarding the best age at which to have this done. Neutering and spaying have proven to be extremely beneficial to male and female puppies, respectively. Besides eliminating the possibility of pregnancy, it inhibits (but does not prevent) breast cancer in bitches and prostate cancer in male dogs.

Your vet should provide your puppy with a thorough dental evaluation at six months of age, ascertaining whether all of the permanent teeth have erupted properly. A home dental-care regimen should be initiated at six months, including brushing weekly and providing good dental

VACCINE ALLERGIES
Vaccines do not work all the time. Sometimes dogs are allergic to them and many times the antibodies, which are supposed to be stimulated by the vaccine, just are not produced. You should keep your dog in the veterinary clinic for an hour after he is vaccinated to be sure there are no allergic reactions.

devices (such as hard plastic or nylon bones). Regular dental care promotes healthy teeth, fresh breath and a longer life.

DOGS OLDER THAN ONE YEAR
Continue to visit the vet at least once a year. There is no such disease as "old age," but bodily functions do change with age. The eyes and ears are no longer as efficient. Liver, kidney and intestinal functions often decline. Proper dietary changes, recommended by your vet, can make life more pleasant for your aging Hovawart and you.

SKIN PROBLEMS
Vets are consulted by dog owners for skin problems more than for any other group of diseases or maladies. A dog's skin is as sensitive, if not more so, than human skin, and both suffer almost the same ailments (though the occurrence of acne in most dogs is rare!). For this reason, veterinary dermatology has developed into a specialty practiced by many vets.

Since many skin problems have visual symptoms that are almost identical, it requires the skill of an experienced veterinary dermatologist to identify and cure many of the more severe skin disorders. Pet shops sell many treatments for skin problems, but most of the treatments are directed at symptoms and not at the underlying problem(s). If your

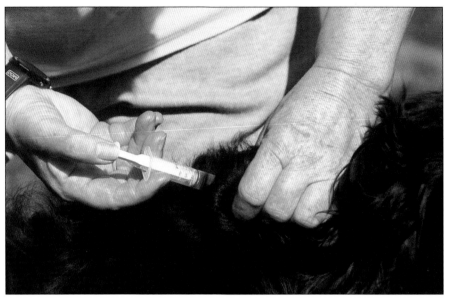

Your vet will manage the details of your Hovawart's vaccinations throughout the dog's life. Most vaccinations are started in puppyhood, usually with annual booster shots in adulthood.

dog is suffering from a skin disorder, you should seek professional assistance as quickly as possible. As with all diseases, the earlier a problem is identified and treated, the more likely it is that the cure will be successful.

HEREDITARY SKIN DISORDERS
Veterinary dermatologists are currently researching a number of skin disorders that are believed to have hereditary bases. These inherited diseases are transmitted by both parents, who appear (phenotypically) normal but have a recessive gene for the disease, meaning that they carry, but are not affected by, the disease. These diseases pose serious problems to breeders because in some instances there are no methods of

identifying carriers. Often the secondary diseases associated with these skin conditions are even more debilitating than the skin disorders themselves, including cancers and respiratory problems.

Among the hereditary skin disorders for which the mode of inheritance is known are acrodermatitis, cutaneous asthenia (Ehlers-Danlos syndrome), sebaceous adenitis, cyclic hematopoiesis, dermatomyositis, IgA deficiency, color dilution alopecia and nodular dermatofibrosis. Some of these disorders are limited to one or two breeds, while others affect a large number of breeds. All inherited diseases must be diagnosed and treated by a veterinary specialist.

PARASITE BITES

Many of us are allergic to insect bites. The bites itch, erupt and may even become infected. Dogs have the same reaction to fleas, ticks and/or mites. When an insect lands on you, you have the chance to whisk it away with your hand. Unfortunately, when a dog is bitten by a flea, tick or mite, he can only scratch it away or bite it. By the time the dog has been bitten, the parasite has done some of its damage. It may also have laid eggs, which will cause further problems in the near future. The itching from parasite bites is probably due to the saliva injected into the site when the parasite sucks the dog's blood.

AIRBORNE ALLERGIES

Just as humans suffer from hay fever during the pollinating season, many dogs suffer from the same allergies. When the pollen count is high, your dog might suffer, but don't expect him to sneeze and have a runny nose as a human would. Dogs react to pollen allergies in the same way they react to fleas—they scratch and bite themselves. Dogs, like humans, can be tested for allergens. Discuss the testing with your vet.

ACRAL LICK GRANULOMA

Many dogs have a very poorly understood syndrome called acral lick granuloma. The manifestation of the problem is the dog's tireless attack at a specific area of the body, almost always the legs or paws. The dog licks so intensively that he removes the hair and skin, leaving an ugly, large wound. Tiny protuberances, which are outgrowths of new capillaries, bead on the surface of the wound. Owners who notice their dogs' biting and chewing at their extremities should have the vet determine the cause. If lick granuloma is identified, although there is no absolute cure, corticosteroids are often used as a treatment.

AUTO-IMMUNE ILLNESSES

An auto-immune illness is one in which the immune system overacts and does not recognize parts of the affected person; rather, the immune system starts to react as if these parts were foreign and need to be destroyed. An example is rheumatoid arthritis, which occurs when the body does not recognize the joints, thus leading to a very painful and damaging reaction in the joints. This has nothing to do with age, so can occur in children. The wear-and-tear arthritis of the older person or dog is osteoarthritis.

Lupus is an auto-immune disease that affects dogs as well as people. It can take variable forms, affecting the kidneys, bones and skin. It can be fatal, so is treated with steroids, which can themselves have very significant side effects. The steroids calm down the allergic reaction to the body's tissues, which helps the lupus, but they also decrease the body's reaction to real foreign substances such as bacteria, and also thin the skin and bone.

FOOD PROBLEMS

Food Allergies

Some dogs can be allergic to many foods that are best-sellers and highly recommended by breeders and vets. Changing the brand of food that you buy may not eliminate the problem if the element to which the dog is allergic is contained in the new brand.

Recognizing a food allergy in a dog can be difficult. Humans often have rashes when they eat foods to which they are allergic, or have swelling of the lips or eyes. Dogs do not usually develop rashes, but react in the same way as they to an airborne or bite allergy—they itch, scratch and bite. While pollen allergies are usually seasonal, food allergies are year-round problems.

Treating Food Allergy

Diagnosis of food allergy is based on a two- to four-week dietary trial with a home-cooked diet fed to the exclusion of all other foods. The diet should consist of boiled rice or potato with a source of protein that the dog has never

eaten before, such as fresh or frozen fish, lamb or even something as exotic as pheasant. Water has to be the only drink, and it is really important that no other foods are fed during this trial. If the dog's condition improves, you will need to try the original diet once again to see if the itching resumes. If it does, then this confirms the diagnosis that the dog is allergic to his original diet. The treatment is long-term feeding

VITAL SIGNS

A dog's normal temperature is 101.5 degrees Fahrenheit. A range of between 100.0 and 102.5 degrees should be considered normal, as each dog's body sets its own temperature. It will be helpful if you take your dog's temperature when you know he is healthy and record it. Then, when you suspect that he is not feeling well, you will have a normal figure to compare the abnormal temperature against.

The normal pulse rate for a dog is between 100 and 125 beats per minute.

of something that does not
distress the dog's skin, which may
be in the form of one of the
commercially available hypoaller-
genic diets or the home-made diet
that you created for the allergy
trial.

FOOD INTOLERANCE
Food intolerance is the inability
of the dog to completely digest
certain foods. This occurs
because the dog does not have
the chemicals necessary to digest
some foodstuffs. These chemicals
are called enzymes. All puppies
have the enzymes necessary to
digest canine milk, but some
dogs do not have the enzymes to
digest a very different form of
milk that is commonly found in
human households—milk from
cows. In such dogs, drinking
cows' milk results in loose
bowels, stomach pains and the
passage of gas.

Dogs often do not have the
enzymes to digest soy or other
beans. The treatment is to
exclude the foodstuffs that upset
your Hovawart's digestion.

BLOAT OR GASTRIC TORSION
This is a problem found in the
deep-chested breeds and is the
subject of much research, but
still manages to take away many
dogs before their time and in a
very horrible way.

A cross-section through a dog
would show how deep the body
cavity is. There are muscles
around the vertebrae that give
strength to the back and allow it
to be flexed and stretched when
running. The stomach hangs like
a handbag with both straps
broken within this deep body
cavity.

There is another way in which
the stomach is held in place.
There is support provided by the
junction with the esophagus or
gullet, and there is support
provided by the junction with the
first part of the small intestine, the
"broken straps of the handbag."
The only other support is a thin
layer of partially opaque "internal
skin" called the peritoneum.

It is no wonder that the stomach can move around easily.
Those breeds with the deepest
chests are at the greatest risk of
having their whole stomachs
twist around (gastric torsion).
This cuts off the blood supply,
prevents the stomach's contents
from leaving and increases the
amount of gas in the stomach.
Once these things have
happened, surgery is vital. If the
blood supply has been cut off too
long and a bit of the stomach
wall dies, death of the dog is
almost inevitable.

The horrendous pain of this
condition is due to the stomach
wall's being stretched by the gas
caught in the stomach, as well as
the stomach wall's desperately
needing the blood that cannot get

to it. There is the pain of not being able to pass a much greater than normal amount of wind; added to this is a pain equivalent to that of a heart attack, which is due to the heart muscle's being starved of blood.

DETECTING BLOAT

The following are symptoms of bloat and require *immediate* veterinary attention:

- Your dog's stomach starts to distend, ending up large and as tight as a football;

TRY TO PREVENT BLOAT

Here are some tips on how to reduce the risk of bloat in your Hovawart:

- Wait at least an hour after exercise before feeding your Hovawart;
- Wait an hour or more after feeding before exercising your Hovawart;
- Do not feed cheap food with high cereal content;
- Feed low-residue diets;
- Elevate food and water bowls to try to reduce any air swallowed;
- If your Hovawart eats quickly, reduce the air swallowed by putting something large and inedible in the food bowl so that the dog has to pick around the object and thus eat more slowly;
- Make sure that the dog is calm and not overly excited or agitated at mealtimes;
- Limit water intake at meals and never allow the dog to gulp water.

- Your dog is dribbling, as no saliva can be swallowed;
- Your dog makes frequent attempts to vomit but cannot bring anything up due to the stomach's being closed off;
- Your dog is distressed from pain;
- Your dog starts to suffer from clinical shock, meaning that there is not enough blood in the dog's circulation as the hard, dilated stomach stops the blood from returning to the heart to be pumped around the body. Clinical shock is indicated by pale gums and tongue, as they have been starved of blood. The shocked dog also has glazed, staring eyes.

You have minutes—yes, *minutes*—to get your dog into surgery. If you see any of these symptoms at any time of the day or night, get to the vet's immediately, where all of the equipment is located. Someone will have to phone and warn that you are on your way (which is a justification for the invention of the cell phone!), so that they can be prepared to get your pet on the operating table right away.

It is possible for a dog to have more than one incident of gastric torsion, even if he has had his stomach stapled, in which the stomach is stapled to the inside of the chest wall to give extra support and prevent its twisting again.

A male dog flea, *Ctenocephalides canis.*

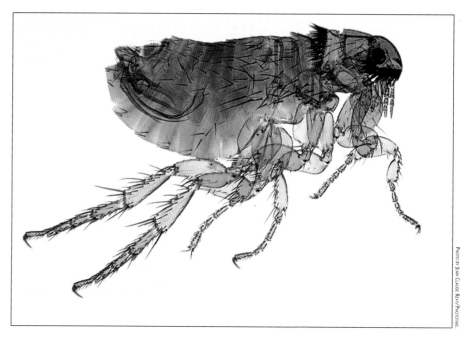

EXTERNAL PARASITES

FLEAS

Of all the problems to which dogs are prone, none is more well known and frustrating than fleas. Flea infestation is relatively simple to cure but difficult to prevent. Parasites that are harbored inside the body are a bit more difficult to eradicate but they are easier to control.

To control flea infestation, you have to understand the flea's life cycle. Fleas are often thought of as a summertime problem, but centrally heated homes have changed the patterns and fleas can be found at any time of the year. The most effective method of flea control is a two-stage approach: one stage to kill the adult fleas, and the other to control the development of pre-adult fleas. Unfortunately, no single active ingredient is effective against all stages of the life cycle.

FLEA KILLER CAUTION— "POISON"

Flea-killers are poisonous. You should not spray these toxic chemicals on areas of a dog's body that he licks, including his genitals and his face. Flea killers taken internally are a better answer, but check with your vet in case internal therapy is not advised for your dog.

LIFE CYCLE STAGES

During its life, a flea will pass through four life stages: egg, larva, pupa or nymph and adult. The adult stage is the most visible and irritating stage of the flea life cycle, and this is why the majority of flea-control products concentrate on this stage. The fact is that adult fleas account for only 1% of the total flea population, and the other 99% exist in pre-adult stages, i.e., eggs, larvae and nymphs. The pre-adult stages are barely visible to the naked eye.

THE LIFE CYCLE OF THE FLEA

Eggs are laid on the dog, usually in quantities of about 20 or 30, several times a day. The adult female flea must have a blood meal before each egg-laying session. When first laid, the eggs will cling to the dog's hair, as the eggs are still moist. However, they will quickly dry out and fall from the dog, especially if the dog moves around or scratches. Many eggs will fall off in the dog's favorite area or an area in which he spends a lot of time, such as his bed.

Once the eggs fall from the dog onto the carpet or furniture, they will hatch into larvae. This takes from one to ten days. Larvae are not particularly mobile and will usually travel only a few inches from where they hatch. However, they do have a tendency to move away from bright light and heavy

EN GARDE:
CATCHING FLEAS OFF GUARD!
Consider the following ways to arm yourself against fleas:
- Add a small amount of pennyroyal or eucalyptus oil to your dog's bath. These natural remedies repel fleas.
- Supplement your dog's food with fresh garlic (minced or grated) and a hearty amount of brewer's yeast, both of which ward off fleas.
- Use a flea comb on your dog daily. Submerge fleas in a cup of bleach to kill them quickly.
- Confine the dog to only a few rooms to limit the spread of fleas in the home.
- Vacuum daily...and get all of the crevices! Dispose of the bag every few days until the problem is under control.
- Wash your dog's bedding daily. Cover cushions where your dog sleeps with towels, and wash the towels often.

traffic—under furniture and behind doors are common places to find high quantities of flea larvae.

The flea larvae feed on dead organic matter, including adult flea feces, until they are ready to change into adult fleas. Fleas will usually remain as larvae for around seven days. After this period, the larvae will pupate into protective pupae. While inside the pupae, the larvae will undergo metamorphosis and change into

Fleas have been measured as being able to jump 300,000 times and can jump 150 times their length in any direction, including straight up.

adult fleas. This can take as little time as a few days, but the adult fleas can remain inside the pupae waiting to hatch for up to two years. The pupae are signaled to hatch by certain stimuli, such as physical pressure—the pupae's being stepped on, heat from an animal's lying on the pupae or increased carbon-dioxide levels and vibrations—indicating that a suitable host is available.

Once hatched, the adult flea must feed within a few days. Once the adult flea finds a host, it will not leave voluntarily. It only becomes dislodged by grooming or the host animal's scratching. The adult flea will remain on the

PHOTO BY DWIGHT R. KUHN

host for the duration of its life unless forcibly removed.

TREATING THE ENVIRONMENT AND THE DOG

Treating fleas should be a two-pronged attack. First, the environment needs to be treated; this includes carpets and furniture, especially the dog's bedding and areas underneath furniture. The environment should be treated with a household spray containing an Insect Growth Regulator (IGR) and an insecticide to kill the adult fleas. Most IGRs are effective against eggs and larvae; they actually mimic the fleas' own hormones and stop the eggs and larvae from developing into adult fleas. There are currently no treatments available to attack the pupa stage of the life cycle, so the adult insecticide is used to kill the newly hatched adult fleas before they find a host. Most IGRs are active for many months, while adult insecticides are only active

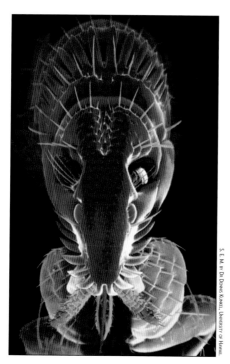

A scanning electron micrograph of a dog or cat flea, *Ctenocephalides*, magnified more than 100x. This image has been colorized for effect.

S. E. M. BY DR DENNIS KUNKEL, UNIVERSITY OF HAWAII.

THE LIFE CYCLE OF THE FLEA

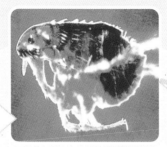

Adult

Egg

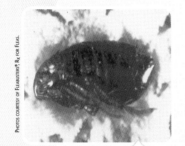

**Pupa
or
Nymph**

Larva

PHOTOS COURTESY OF FLEABUSTERS® RX FOR FLEAS.

Fleas have been around for millions of years and have adapted to changing host animals. They are able to go through a complete life cycle in less than one month or they can extend their lives to almost two years by remaining as pupae or cocoons. They do not need blood or any other food for up to 20 months.

> ### INSECT GROWTH REGULATOR (IGR)
> Two types of products should be used when treating fleas—a product to treat the pet and a product to treat the home. Adult fleas represent less than 1% of the flea population. The pre-adult fleas (eggs, larvae and pupae) represent more than 99% of the flea population and are found in the environment; it is in the case of pre-adult fleas that products containing an Insect Growth Regulator (IGR) should be used in the home.
>
> IGRs are a new class of compounds used to prevent the development of insects. They do not kill the insect outright, but instead use the insect's biology against it to stop it from completing its growth. Products that contain methoprene are the world's first and leading IGRs. Used to control fleas and other insects, this type of IGR will stop flea larvae from developing and protect the house for up to seven months.

The American dog tick, *Dermacentor variabilis*, is probably the most common tick found on dogs. Look at the strength in its eight legs! No wonder it's hard to detach them.

for a few days.

When treating with a household spray, it is a good idea to vacuum before applying the product. This stimulates as many pupae as possible to hatch into adult fleas. The vacuum cleaner should also be treated with an insecticide to prevent the eggs and larvae that have been collected in the vacuum bag from hatching.

The second stage of treatment is to apply an adult insecticide to the dog. Traditionally, this would be in the form of a collar or a spray, but more recent innovations include digestible insecticides that poison the fleas when they ingest the dog's blood. Alternatively, there are drops that, when placed on the back of the dog's neck, spread throughout the hair and skin to kill adult fleas.

TICKS
Though not as common as fleas, ticks are found all over the tropical and temperate world. They don't bite, like fleas; they harpoon. They dig their sharp proboscis (nose) into the dog's skin and drink the blood. Their only food and drink is dog's

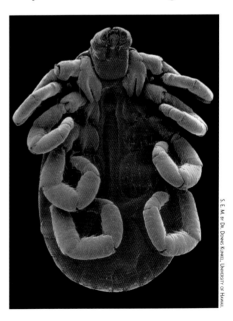

blood. Dogs can get Lyme disease, Rocky Mountain spotted fever, tick bite paralysis and many other diseases from ticks. They may live where fleas are found and they like to hide in cracks or seams in walls. They are controlled the same way fleas are controlled.

The American dog tick, *Dermacentor variabilis*, may well be the most common dog tick in many geographical areas, especially those areas where the climate is hot and humid. Most dog ticks have life expectancies of a week to six months, depending upon climatic conditions. They can neither jump nor fly, but they can crawl slowly and can range up to 16 feet to reach a sleeping or unsuspecting dog.

MITES

Just as fleas and ticks can be problematic for your dog, mites can also lead to an itchy nuisance. Microscopic in size, mites are related to ticks and generally take up permanent residence on their host animal—in this case, your dog! The term *mange* refers to any infestation caused by one of the mighty mites, of which there are six varieties that concern dog owners.

Demodex mites cause a condition known as demodicosis (sometimes called red mange or

DEER-TICK CROSSING

The great outdoors may be fun for your dog, but it also is an home to dangerous ticks. Deer ticks carry a bacterium known as *Borrelia burgdorferi* and are most active in the autumn and spring. When infections are caught early, penicillin and tetracycline are effective antibiotics, but, if left untreated, the bacteria may cause neurological, kidney and cardiac problems as well as long-term trouble with walking and painful joints.

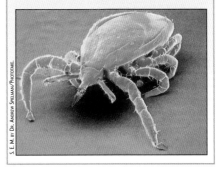

S. E. M. BY DR. ANDREW SPIELMAN/PHOTOTAKE.

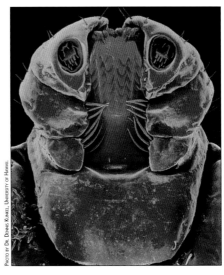

PHOTO BY DR. DENNIS KUNKEL, UNIVERSITY OF HAWAII.

The head of an American dog tick, *Dermacentor variabilis*, enlarged and colorized for effect.

The mange mite,
Psoroptes bovis,
can infest cattle
and other
domestic animals.

PHOTO BY JAMES HAYDEN/YOAV/PHOTOTAKE

follicular mange), in which the mites live in the dog's hair follicles and sebaceous glands in larger-than-normal numbers. This type of mange is commonly passed from the dam to her puppies and usually shows up on the puppies' muzzles, though demodicosis is not transferable from one normal dog to another. Most dogs recover from this type of mange without any treatment, though topical therapies are commonly prescribed by the vet.

Human lice look
like dog lice;
the two are
closely related.
PHOTO BY DWIGHT R. KUHN.

The *Cheyletiellosis* mite is the hook-mouthed culprit associated with "walking dandruff," a condition that affects dogs as well as cats and rabbits. This mite lives on the surface of the animal's skin and is readily transferable through direct or indirect contact with an affected animal. The dandruff is present in the form of scaly skin, which may or may not be itchy. If not treated, this mange can affect a whole kennel of dogs and can be spread to humans as well.

The *Sarcoptes* mite causes intense itching on the dog in the form of a condition known as scabies or sarcoptic mange. The cycle of the *Sarcoptes* mite lasts about three weeks, and the mites live in the top layer of the dog's skin (epidermis), preferably in areas with little hair. Scabies is highly contagious and can be passed to humans. Sometimes an allergic reaction to the mite worsens the severe itching associated with sarcoptic mange.

Ear mites, *Otodectes cynotis,* lead to otodectic mange, which most commonly affects the outer ear canal of the dog, though other areas can be affected as well. Dogs with ear-mite infestation commonly scratch at their ears, causing further irritation, and shake their heads. Dark brown droppings in the outer ear confirm the diagnosis. Your vet can prescribe a treatment to flush out the ears and kill any eggs in the ears. A complete month of treatment is necessary to cure the mange.

Two other mites, less common in dogs, include *Dermanyssus gallinae* (the poultry or red mite) and *Eutrombicula alfreddugesi* (the North American mite associated with trombiculidiasis or chigger infestation). The poultry mite frequently lives on chickens, but can transfer to dogs who spend time near farm animals. Chigger infestation affects dogs in the

DO NOT MIX
Never mix parasite-control products without first consulting your vet. Some products can become toxic when combined with others and can cause fatal consequences.

NOT A DROP TO DRINK
Never allow your dog to swim in polluted water or public areas where water quality can be suspect. Even perfectly clear water can harbor parasites, many of which can cause serious to fatal illnesses in canines. Areas inhabited by waterfowl and other wildlife are especially dangerous.

Central US who have exposure to woodlands. The types of mange caused by both of these mites are treatable by vets.

INTERNAL PARASITES
Most animals—fishes, birds and mammals, including dogs and humans—have worms and other parasites that live inside their bodies. According to Dr. Herbert R. Axelrod, the fish pathologist, there are two kinds of parasites: dumb and smart. The smart parasites live in peaceful cooperation with their hosts (symbiosis), while the dumb parasites kill their hosts. Most worm infections are relatively easy to control. If they are not controlled, they weaken the host dog to the point that other medical problems occur, but they do not kill the host as dumb parasites would.

A brown dog tick, *Rhipicephalus sanguineus*, is an uncommon but annoying tick found on dogs. PHOTO BY CAROLINA BIOLOGICAL SUPPLY/PHOTOTAKE.

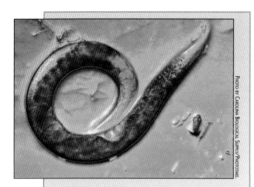

PHOTO BY CAROLINA BIOLOGICAL SUPPLY/PHOTOTAKE.

The roundworm *Rhabditis* can infect both dogs and humans.

ROUNDWORMS

Average-size dogs can pass 1,360,000 roundworm eggs every day. For example, if there were only 1 million dogs in the world, the world would be saturated with thousands of tons of dog feces. These feces would contain around 15,000,000,000 roundworm eggs.

Up to 31% of home yards and children's sand boxes in the US contain roundworm eggs.

Flushing dog's feces down the toilet is not a safe practice because the usual sewage treatments do not destroy roundworm eggs.

Infected puppies start shedding roundworm eggs at three weeks of age. They can be infected by their mother's milk.

The roundworm, *Ascaris lumbricoides.*

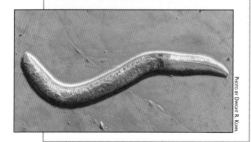

PHOTO BY DWIGHT R. KUHN.

ROUNDWORMS

The roundworms that infect dogs are known scientifically as *Toxocara canis*. They live in the dog's intestines and shed eggs continually. It has been estimated that a dog produces about 6 or more ounces of feces every day. Each ounce of feces averages hundreds of thousands of roundworm eggs. There are no known areas in which dogs roam that do not contain roundworm eggs. The greatest danger of roundworms is that they infect people, too! It is wise to have your dog tested regularly for roundworms.

In young puppies, roundworms cause bloated bellies, diarrhea, coughing and vomiting, and are transmitted from the dam (through blood or milk). Affected puppies will not appear as animated as normal puppies. The worms appear spaghetti-like, measuring as long as 6 inches. Adult dogs can acquire roundworms through coprophagia (eating contaminated feces) or by killing rodents that carry roundworms.

Roundworm infection can kill puppies and cause severe problems in adults, as the hatched larvae travel to the lungs and trachea through the bloodstream. Cleanliness is the best preventative for roundworms. Always pick up after your dog and dispose of feces in appropriate receptacles.

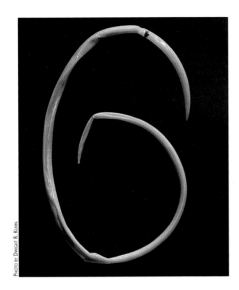

The hookworm, *Ancylostoma caninum.*

HOOKWORMS

In the United States, dog owners have to be concerned about four different species of hookworm, the most common and most serious of which is *Ancylostoma caninum,* which prefers warm climates. The others are *Ancylostoma braziliense, Ancylostoma tubaeforme* and *Uncinaria stenocephala,* the latter of which is a concern to dogs living in the Northern US and Canada, as this species prefers cold climates. Hookworms are dangerous to humans as well as to dogs and cats, and can be the cause of severe anemia due to iron deficiency. The worm uses its teeth to attach itself to the dog's intestines and changes the site of its attachment about six times per day. Each time the worm repositions itself, the dog loses blood and can become anemic. *Ancylostoma caninum* is the most likely of the four species to cause anemia in the dog.

Symptoms of hookworm infection include dark stools, weight loss, general weakness, pale coloration and anemia, as well as possible skin problems. Fortunately, hookworms are easily purged from the affected dog with a number of medications that have proven effective. Discuss these with your vet. Most heartworm preventatives include a hookworm insecticide as well.

Owners also must be aware that hookworms can infect humans, who can acquire the larvae through exposure to contaminated feces. Since the worms cannot complete their life cycle on a human, the worms simply infest the skin and cause irritation. This condition is known as cutaneous larva migrans syndrome. As a preventative, use disposable gloves or a "poop-scoop" to pick up your dog's droppings and prevent your dog (or neighborhood cats) from defecating in children's play areas.

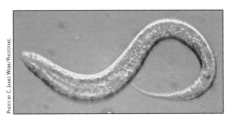

The infective stage of the hookworm larva.

TAPEWORMS

Humans, rats, squirrels, foxes, coyotes, wolves and domestic dogs are all susceptible to tapeworm infection. Except in humans, tapeworms are usually not a fatal infection. Infected individuals can harbor 1000 parasitic worms.

Tapeworms, like some other types of worm, are hermaphroditic, meaning male and female in the same worm.

If dogs eat infected rats or mice, or anything else infected with tapeworm, they get the tapeworm disease. One month after attaching to a dog's intestine, the worm starts shedding eggs. These eggs are infective immediately. Infective eggs can live for a few months without a host animal.

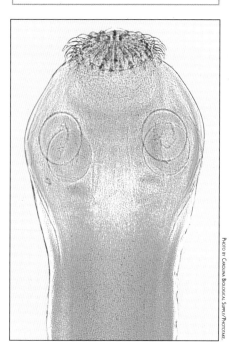

The head and rostellum (the round prominence on the scolex) of a tapeworm, which infects dogs and humans.

PHOTO BY CAROLINA BIOLOGICAL SUPPLY/PHOTOTAKE.

TAPEWORMS

There are many species of tapeworm, all of which are carried by fleas! The most common tapeworm affecting dogs is known as *Dipylidium caninum*. The dog eats the flea and starts the tapeworm cycle. Humans can also be infected with tapeworms—so don't eat fleas! Fleas are so small that your dog could pass them onto your hands, your plate or your food and thus make it possible for you to ingest a flea that is carrying tapeworm eggs.

While tapeworm infection is not life-threatening in dogs (smart parasite!), it can be the cause of a very serious liver disease for humans. About 50% of the humans infected with *Echinococcus multilocularis*, a type of tapeworm that causes alveolar hydatid, perish.

WHIPWORMS

In North America, whipworms are counted among the most common parasitic worms in dogs. The whipworm's scientific name is *Trichuris vulpis*. These worms attach themselves in the lower parts of the intestine, where they feed. Affected dogs may only experience upset tummies, colic and diarrhea. These worms, however, can live for months or years in the dog, beginning their larval stage in the small intestine, spending their adult stage in the large intestine and finally passing infective eggs through the dog's feet. The only way to detect whipworms is through a fecal examination, though this is not always foolproof. Treatment for whipworms is tricky, due to the worms' unusual life-cycle pattern, and very often dogs are reinfected due to exposure to infective eggs on the ground. The whipworm eggs can survive in the environment for as long as five years; thus, cleaning up droppings in your own backyard as well as in public places is absolutely essential for sanitation purposes and the health of your dog and others.

THREADWORMS
Though less common than round-worms, hookworms and those previously mentioned, thread-worms concern dog owners in the Southwestern US and Gulf Coast area where the climate is hot and humid. Living in the small intes-tine of the dog, this worm meas-ures a mere 2 millimeters and is round in shape. Like that of the whipworm, the threadworm's life cycle is very complex and the eggs and larvae are passed through the feces. A deadly disease in humans, *Strongyloides* readily infects people, and the handling of feces is the most common means of trans-mission. Threadworms are most often seen in young puppies; bloody diarrhea and pneumonia are symptoms. Sick puppies must be isolated and treated immedi-ately; vets recommend a follow-up treatment one month later.

HEARTWORM PREVENTATIVES

There are many heartworm preventatives on the market, many of which are sold at your veterinarian's office. These products can be given daily or monthly, depending on the manufacturer's instructions. All of these preventatives contain chemical insecticides directed at killing heartworms, which leads to some controversy among dog owners. In effect, heartworm preventatives are neces-sary evils, though you should determine how necessary based on your pet's lifestyle. There is no doubt that heartworm is a dreadful disease that threatens the lives of dogs. However, the likelihood of your dog's being bitten by an infected mosquito is slim in most places, and a mosquito-repellent (or an herbal remedy such as Wormwood or Black Walnut) is much safer for your dog and will not compromise his immune system (the way heartworm preventatives will). Should you decide to use the tradi-tional preventative "medications," you can consider giving the pill every other or third month. Since the toxins in the pill will kill the heartworms at all stages of develop-ment, the pill would be effective in killing larvae, nymphs or adults and it takes four months for the larvae to reach the adult stage. Thus, there is no rationale to poison-ing the dog's system on a monthly basis. Lastly, do not give the pill during the winter months, since there are no mosquitoes around to pass on their infection, unless you live in a tropical environment.

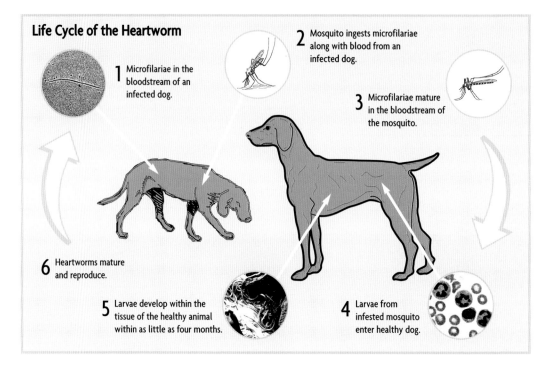

Life Cycle of the Heartworm

1 Microfilariae in the bloodstream of an infected dog.

2 Mosquito ingests microfilariae along with blood from an infected dog.

3 Microfilariae mature in the bloodstream of the mosquito.

6 Heartworms mature and reproduce.

5 Larvae develop within the tissue of the healthy animal within as little as four months.

4 Larvae from infested mosquito enter healthy dog.

HEARTWORMS

Heartworms are thin, extended worms up to 12 inches long, which live in a dog's heart and the major blood vessels surrounding it. Dogs may have up to 200 worms. Symptoms may be loss of energy, loss of appetite, coughing, the development of a pot belly and anemia.

Heartworms are transmitted by mosquitoes. The mosquito drinks the blood of an infected dog and takes in larvae with the blood. The larvae, called microfilariae, develop within the body of the mosquito and are passed on to the next dog bitten after the larvae mature. It takes two to three weeks for the larvae to develop to the infective stage within the body of the mosquito. Dogs are usually treated at about six weeks of age and maintained on a prophylactic dose given monthly.

Blood testing for heartworms is not necessarily indicative of how seriously your dog is infected. Although this is a dangerous disease, it is not easy for a dog to be infected. Discuss the various preventatives with your vet, as there are many different types now available. Together you can decide on a safe course of prevention for your dog.

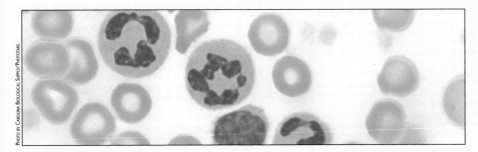

Magnified heartworm larvae, *Dirofilaria immitis.*

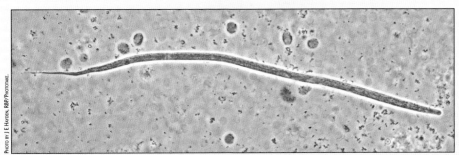

Heartworm, *Dirofilaria immitis.*

The heart of a dog infected with canine heartworm, *Dirofilaria immitis.*

HOMEOPATHY:
an alternative
to conventional
medicine

"Less is Most"

Using this principle, the strength of a homeopathic remedy is measured by the number of serial dilutions that were undertaken to create it. The greater the number of serial dilutions, the greater the strength of the homeopathic remedy. The potency of a remedy that has been made by making a dilution of 1 part in 100 parts (or 1/100) is 1c or 1cH. If this remedy is subjected to a series of further dilutions, each one being 1/100, a more dilute and stronger remedy is produced. If the remedy is diluted in this way six times, it is called 6c or 6cH. A dilution of 6c is 1 part in 1,000,000,000,000. In general, higher potencies in more frequent doses are better for acute symptoms and lower potencies in more infrequent doses are more useful for chronic, long-standing problems.

CURING OUR DOGS NATURALLY

Holistic medicine means treating the whole animal as a unique, perfect living being. Generally, holistic treatments do not suppress the symptoms that the body naturally produces, as do most medications prescribed by conventional doctors and vets. Holistic methods seek to cure disease by regaining balance and harmony in the patient's environment. Some of these methods include use of nutritional therapy, herbs, flower essences, aromatherapy, acupuncture, massage, chiropractic and, of course, the most popular holistic approach, homeopathy.

Homeopathy is a theory or system of treating illness with small doses of substances which, if administered in larger quantities, would produce the symptoms that the patient already has. This approach is often described as "like cures like." Although modern veterinary medicine is geared toward the "quick fix," homeopathy relies on the belief that, given the time, the body is able to heal itself and return to its natural, healthy state.

Choosing a remedy to cure a problem in our dogs is the difficult part of homeopathy. Consult with your vet for a professional diagnosis of your dog's symptoms. Often these symptoms require immediate conventional care. If your vet is willing and knowledgeable, you may attempt a homeopathic remedy. Be aware that cortisone prevents homeopathic remedies from working. There are hundreds of possibilities and combinations to cure many problems in dogs, from basic physical problems such as excessive shedding, fleas or other parasites, unattractive doggy odor, bad breath, upset tummy, obesity, dry, oily or dull coat, diarrhea, ear problems or eye discharge (including tears and dry or mucousy matter), to behavioral abnormalities such as fear of loud noises, habitual licking, poor appetite, excessive barking and various phobias. From alumina to zincum metallicum, the remedies span the planet and the imagination…from flowers and weeds to chemicals, insect droppings, diesel smoke and volcanic ash.

Using "Like to Treat Like"

Unlike conventional medicines that suppress symptoms, homeopathic remedies treat illnesses with small doses of substances that, if administered in larger quantities, would produce the symptoms that the patient already has. While the same homeopathic remedy can be used to treat different symptoms in different dogs, here are some interesting remedies and their uses.

Apis Mellifica
(made from honey bee venom) can be used for allergies or to reduce swelling that occurs in acutely infected kidneys.

Diesel Smoke
can be used to help control travel sickness.

Calcarea Fluorica
(made from calcium fluoride, which helps harden bone structure) can be useful in treating hard lumps in tissues.

Natrum Muriaticum
(made from common salt, sodium chloride) is useful in treating thin, thirsty dogs.

Nitricum Acidum
(made from nitric acid) is used for symptoms you would expect to see from contact with acids, such as lesions, especially where the skin joins the linings of body orifices or openings such as the lips and nostrils.

Symphytum
(made from the herb Knitbone, *Symphytum officinale*) is used to encourage bones to heal.

Urtica Urens
(made from the common stinging nettle) is used in treating painful, irritating rashes.

First Aid at a Glance

Burns
Place the affected area under cool water; use ice if only a small area is burnt.

Bee stings/Insect bites
Apply ice to relieve swelling; antihistamine dosed properly.

Animal bites
Clean any bleeding area; apply pressure until bleeding subsides; go to the vet.

Spider bites
Use cold compress and a pressurized pack to inhibit venom's spreading.

Antifreeze poisoning
Induce vomiting with hydrogen peroxide. Seek *immediate* veterinary help!

Fish hooks
Removal best handled by vet; hook must be cut in order to remove.

Snake bites
Pack ice around bite; contact vet quickly; identify snake for proper antivenin.

Car accident
Move dog from roadway with blanket; seek veterinary aid.

Shock
Calm the dog; keep him warm; seek immediate veterinary help.

Nosebleed
Apply cold compress to the nose; apply pressure to any visible abrasion.

Bleeding
Apply pressure above the area; treat wound by applying a cotton pack.

Heat stroke
Submerge dog in cold bath; cool down with fresh air and water; go to the vet.

Frostbite/Hypothermia
Warm the dog with a warm bath, electric blankets or hot water bottles.

Abrasions
Clean the wound and wash out thoroughly with fresh water; apply antiseptic.

 Remember: an injured dog may attempt to bite a helping hand from fear and confusion. Always muzzle the dog before trying to offer assistance.

Number-One Killer Disease in Dogs: CANCER

In every age, there is a word associated with a disease or plague that causes humans to shudder. In the 21st century, that word is "cancer." Just as cancer is the leading cause of death in humans, it claims nearly half the lives of dogs that die from a natural disease as well as half the dogs that die over the age of ten years.

Described as a genetic disease, cancer becomes a greater risk as the dog ages. Veterinarians and dog owners have become increasingly aware of the threat of cancer to dogs. Statistics reveal that one dog in every five will develop cancer, the most common of which is skin cancer. Many cancers, including prostate, ovarian and breast cancer, can be avoided by spaying and neutering our dogs by the age of six months.

Early detection of cancer can save or extend your dog's life, so it is absolutely vital for owners to have their dogs examined by a qualified vet or oncologist immediately upon detection of any abnormality. Certain dietary guidelines have also proven to reduce the onset and spread of cancer. Foods based on fish rather than beef, due to the presence of Omega-3 fatty acids, are recommended. Other amino acids such as glutamine have significant benefits for canines, particularly those breeds that show a greater susceptibility to cancer.

Cancer management and treatments promise hope for future generations of canines. Since the disease is genetic, breeders should never breed a dog whose parents, grandparents and any related siblings have developed cancer. It is difficult to know whether to exclude an otherwise healthy dog from a breeding program as the disease does not manifest itself until the dog's senior years.

RECOGNIZE CANCER WARNING SIGNS

Since early detection can possibly rescue your dog from becoming a cancer statistic, it is essential for owners to recognize the possible signs and seek the assistance of a qualified professional.

• Abnormal bumps or lumps that continue to grow
• Bleeding or discharge from any body cavity
• Persistent stiffness or lameness
• Recurrent sores or sores that do not heal
• Inappetence
• Breathing difficulties
• Weight loss
• Bad breath or odors
• General malaise and fatigue
• Eating and swallowing problems
• Difficulty urinating and defecating

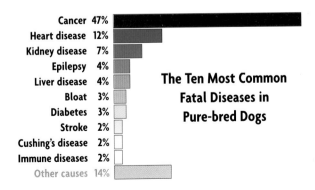

Cancer	47%
Heart disease	12%
Kidney disease	7%
Epilepsy	4%
Liver disease	4%
Bloat	3%
Diabetes	3%
Stroke	2%
Cushing's disease	2%
Immune diseases	2%
Other causes	14%

The Ten Most Common Fatal Diseases in Pure-bred Dogs

HOVAWART

The term *old* is a qualitative term. For dogs, as well as for their masters, old is relative. Certainly we can all distinguish between a puppy Hovawart and an adult Hovawart—there are the obvious physical traits, such as size, appearance and facial expressions, as well as personality traits. Puppies and young dogs like to play with children. Children's natural exuberance is a good match for the seemingly endless energy of young dogs. They like to run, jump, chase and retrieve. When dogs grow older and cease their interaction with children, they are often thought of as being too old to keep pace with the children. On the other hand, if a Hovawart is only exposed to people with quieter lifestyles, his life will normally be less active and the decrease in his activity level as he ages will not be as obvious.

If people live to be 100 years old, dogs live to be 20 years old. While this might seem like a good rule of thumb, it is very inaccurate. When trying to compare dog years to human years, you cannot make a generalization about all dogs. You can make the generalization that Hovawarts live to be around 13 or 14 years of age and, as with every living creature, the Hovawart ages. This aging is apparent usually after the dog reaches 10 years of age.

Dogs in general are considered physically mature at three years of age (or earlier), but can reproduce even earlier. So the first three years of a dog's life are like seven times that of comparable humans. That means a 3-year-old dog is like a 21-year-old human. As the curve of comparison shows, there is no hard-and-fast rule for comparing dog and human ages. Small breeds tend to live longer than large breeds, some breeds' adolescent periods last longer than others' and some breeds experience rapid periods of growth. The comparison is made even more difficult, for, likewise, not all humans age at the same rate...and human females live longer than human males.

WHAT TO LOOK FOR IN SENIORS

Most vets and behaviorists use the seven-year mark as the time to consider a dog a senior in terms of changes in veterinary care. This term does not imply that the dog is geriatric and has begun to fail in mind and body. Aging is essentially a slowing process. Humans readily admit that they feel a difference in their activity level from age 20 to 30, and then from 30 to 40, etc. By treating the seven-year-old dog as a senior, owners are able to implement certain therapeutic and preventative medical strategies with the help of their vets.

A special-care program should include at least two veterinary visits per year and screening sessions to determine the dog's health status, as well as nutritional counseling. Vets determine a senior dog's health status through a blood smear for a complete blood count, serum chemistry profile with electrolytes, urinalysis, blood pressure check, electrocardiogram, ocular tonometry (pressure on the eyeball) and dental prophylaxis.

Such an extensive program for senior dogs is well advised before owners start to see the obvious physical signs of aging, such as slower and inhibited movement, graying, increased sleep/nap periods and disinterest in play and other activity. This preventative program promises a longer, healthier life for the aging dog. Among the physical problems common in aging dogs are the loss of sight and hearing, arthritis,

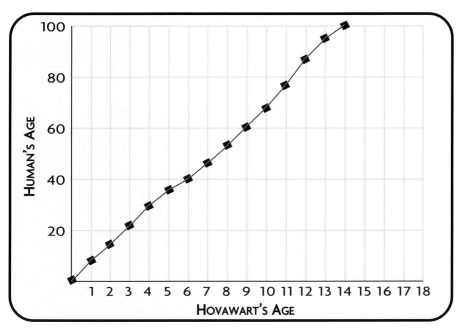

kidney and liver failure, diabetes mellitus, heart disease and Cushing's disease (a hormonal disease).

In addition to the physical manifestations discussed, there are some behavioral changes and problems related to aging dogs. Dogs suffering from hearing or vision loss, dental discomfort or arthritis can become aggressive. Likewise, the near-deaf and/or blind dog may be startled more easily and react in an unexpectedly aggressive manner. Senior dogs suffering from senility can become more impatient and irritable. Potty accidents are associated with loss of mobility, kidney problems and loss of sphincter control as well as plaque accumulation, physiological brain changes and reactions to medications. Older dogs, just like young puppies, suffer from separation anxiety, which can lead to excessive barking, whining, housesoiling and destructive behavior. Aging dogs may become fearful of everyday sounds, such as vacuum cleaners, heaters, thunder and passing traffic. Some may have difficulty sleeping, due to discomfort, the need for frequent toilet visits and the like.

Owners should avoid spoiling the older dog with too many treats. Obesity is a common problem in older dogs and subtracts years from their lives. Keep the senior dog as trim as possible,

---

NOTICING THE SYMPTOMS

The symptoms listed below are symptoms that gradually appear and become more noticeable. They are not life-threatening; however, the symptoms below are to be taken very seriously and warrant a discussion with your vet:

- Your dog cries and whimpers when he moves, and he stops running completely.
- Convulsions start or become more serious and frequent. The usual convulsion (spasm) is when the dog stiffens and starts to tremble, being unable or unwilling to move. The seizure usually lasts for 5 to 30 minutes.
- Your dog drinks more water and urinates more frequently. Wetting and bowel accidents take place indoors without warning.
- Vomiting becomes more and more frequent.

---

since excessive weight puts additional stress on the body's vital organs. Some breeders recommend supplementing the diet with foods high in fiber and lower in calories. Adding fresh vegetables and marrow broth to the senior's diet makes a tasty, low-calorie, low-fat supplement. Vets also offer specialty diets for senior dogs that are worth exploring.

Your dog, as he nears his twilight years, needs your patience and good care more than ever. Never punish an older dog for an accident or abnormal behavior. For all the years of love, protection and companionship that your dog has provided, he deserves special attention and courtesies. The older dog may need to relieve himself at 3 a.m. because he can no longer "hold it" for eight hours. Older dogs may not be able to remain crated for more than two or three hours. It may be time to give up a sofa or chair to your old friend. Although he may not seem as enthusiastic about your attention and petting, he does appreciate the considerations you offer as he gets older.

Your Hovawart does not understand why his world is slowing down. Owners must make their dogs' transition into their golden years as pleasant and rewarding as possible.

WHEN THE TIME COMES

You are never fully prepared to make a rational decision about putting your dog to sleep. It is very obvious that you love your Hovawart or you would not be reading this book. Putting a beloved dog to sleep is extremely difficult. It is a decision that must be made with your vet. You are usually forced to make the decision when your dog experiences one or more life-threatening symptoms that have become serious enough for you to seek veterinary assistance.

If the prognosis of the malady indicates that the end is near and that your beloved pet will only continue to suffer and experience no enjoyment for the balance of his life, then euthanasia is the right choice.

Three generations of vibrant-looking Hovawarts...it's difficult to tell who's older! From left to right: Azina Lemania Denges (11 years old); Ozane-Jinka des Trois Petits Diables (2 years old); Jinka des Trois Petits Diables (5 years old).

COPING WITH LOSS

When your dog dies, you may be as upset as when a human companion passes away. You are losing your protector, your baby, your confidante and your best friend. Many people experience not only grief but also feelings of guilt and doubt as to whether they did all that they could for their pet. Allow yourself to grieve and mourn, and seek help from friends and support groups. You may also wish to consult books and websites that deal with this topic.

WHAT IS EUTHANASIA?

Euthanasia derives from the Greek, meaning *good death*. In other words, it means the planned, painless killing of a dog suffering from a painful, incurable condition, or who is so aged that he cannot walk, see, eat or control his excretory functions. Euthanasia is usually accomplished by injection with an overdose of anesthesia or a barbiturate. Aside from the prick of the needle, the experience is usually painless. Your vet will help with making the decision, and you may be allowed to accompany your dog during the procedure, allowing your friend to go to sleep in your arms.

MAKING THE DECISION

The decision to euthanize your dog is never easy. The days during which the dog becomes ill and the end occurs can be unusually stressful for you. If this is your first experience with the death of a loved one, you may need the comfort dictated by your religious beliefs. If you are the head of the family and have children, you

There are cemeteries for deceased pets. Consult your vet to help find one in your area.

should have involved them in the decision of putting your Hovawart to sleep. Usually your dog can be maintained on drugs for a few days in order to give you ample time to make a decision. During this time, talking with members of your family or with people who have lived through the same experience can ease the burden of your inevitable decision.

THE FINAL RESTING PLACE

Dogs can have some of the same privileges as humans. The remains of your beloved dog can be buried in a pet cemetery, which is generally expensive. If your dog has died at home, he can be buried in your yard in a suitable spot marked by a stone, flowers or a newly planted tree, except in places where home burials are prohibited by law.

Alternatively, your dog can be cremated individually and the ashes returned to you. A less expensive option is mass cremation, although, of course, the ashes cannot then be returned. Vets can usually help you locate a pet cemetery or arrange the cremation on your behalf. The cost of these options should always be discussed frankly and openly with your vet.

GETTING ANOTHER DOG?

The grief of losing your beloved dog will be as lasting as the grief of losing a human friend or relative. In most cases, if your dog died of old age (if there is such a thing), he had slowed down considerably. Do you want a new Hovawart puppy to replace him? Or are you better off finding a more mature Hovawart, say two to three years of age, which will usually be house-trained and will have an already developed personality. In this case, you can find out if you like each other after a few hours of being together.

The decision is, of course, your own. Do you want another Hovawart or perhaps a different breed so as to avoid comparison with your beloved friend? Most people usually stay with the same breed because they know (and love) the characteristics of that breed. Remember the best moments that you and your Hovawart spent together, conscious of the fact that it will ease your grief and that your experience will help you with your new Hovawart. You may even know some other Hovawart people and perhaps you are lucky enough that a breeder you respect expects a litter soon.

TALK IT OUT

The more openly your family discusses the whole stressful occurrence of the aging and eventual loss of a beloved pet, the easier it will be for you when the time comes.

SHOWING YOUR
HOVAWART

When you purchase your Hovawart, you will make it clear to the breeder whether you want one just as a lovable companion and pet, or if you hope to be buying a Hovawart with show prospects. No reputable breeder will sell you a young puppy and tell you that it is *definitely* of show quality, for so much can go wrong during the early months of a puppy's development. If you plan to show, what you will hopefully have acquired is a puppy with "show potential."

If you seek to turn your Hovawart into a show dog, you should begin training early to ensure that he learns how to behave. First, when the puppy is not distracted and is comfortable with you, teach him in the form of a game to allow his teeth to be shown and to be touched all over his body, as the judge will examine the dog physically for correct structure. Do this exercise regularly and, once the dog has become comfortable with it, ask strangers to perform the same exercise until the dog finds it to be natural.

You will need to teach the dog to gait properly on the lead, always keeping him on your left. You should begin this training at home and then progress to practicing in areas unfamiliar to the pup, although always without distraction. The dog will need to trot without jumping or pulling on the lead, and will need to hold his head proudly up. The Hovawart is naturally proud and holds his head well, but show ring posture can be practiced and perfected with the aid of a treat to get your Hovawart's attention.

With this basic training at home, your Hovawart should be ready for showing and you will be more relaxed and at ease. Judges will notice this, and your confidence in the ring gains points in the long run.

The first concept that the canine novice learns when watching a dog show is that each dog first competes against members of its own breed. Once the judge has selected the best member of each breed (Best of Breed), provided that the show is judged on a Group system, that chosen dog will compete with other dogs in its group. Finally, the dogs chosen first in each group will compete for Best in Show.

The second concept that you must understand is that the dogs are not actually compared against one another. The judge compares each dog against its breed standard. While some early breed standards were indeed based on specific dogs that were famous or popular, many dedicated enthusiasts say that a perfect specimen, as described in the standard, has never walked into a show ring, has never been bred and, to the woe of dog breeders around the globe, does not exist. Breeders attempt to get as close to this ideal as possible with every litter, but theoretically the "perfect" dog is so elusive that it is impossible.

If you are interested in exploring the world of dog showing, your best bet is to join your local breed club or the national parent club. These clubs often host both regional and national specialties, shows only for Hovawarts, which can include conformation as well as obedience trials. Even if you have no intention of competing with your Hovawart, a specialty is like a festival for lovers of the breed who congregate to share their favorite topic: Hovawarts! Clubs also send out newsletters, and some organize training days and seminars in order that people may learn more about their chosen breed.

Each year, every Hovawart club organizes what is called a "National Breeding" get-together. The aim is to attract as many people as possible that represent Hovawart breeders and owners, as well as to discuss the evolution of the breed, to perform different behavioral tests and to select the best breeding stock or future breeding stock, based on the physical conformation, behavior and genetics of the Hovawarts available.

If your Hovawart is of age and registered, you can enter him in a dog show where the breed is offered classes. Only unaltered dogs can be entered in a dog show, so if you have spayed or neutered your Hovawart, he or she cannot compete in conformation shows. The reason for this is simple. Dog shows are the main forum to prove which representatives of a breed are worthy of being bred. Only dogs that have achieved championships— the recognized "seal of approval"

Nalko des Trois Petits Diables, owned by Mr. Descampes, in the show ring.

CLASSES AT FCI SHOWS
- Puppy Class: 6–9 months, without grading;
- Novice Class: 9–12 months; possible appraisals: Somewhat Promising, Promising, Very Promising;
- Youth Class: 12–18 months; possible appraisals: Poor, Fair, Good, Very Good, Excellent;
- Open Class: As of 15 months; possible appraisals are the same as the Youth Class. This class can also provide the dog with the CAC for national competitions in concurrence with the Work Class and the CACIB for international competitions in concurrence with the Working and Champion Classes;
- Work Class: 15 months minimum. Same qualifications as the Open Class but the dog must hold a Work Dog title;
- Champion Class: 15 months minimum. Reserved for holders of national and international titles only. This class can obtain the same qualifications as the Open Class but can only be awarded the CACIB.

first time in the ring, do not be over-anxious and run to the front of the line. It is much better to stand back and study how the exhibitor in front of you is performing. The judge asks each handler to "stack" the dog, hopefully showing the dog off to his best advantage. The judge will observe the dog from a distance and from different angles, and approach the dog to check his teeth, overall structure, alertness and muscle tone, as well as consider how well the dog "conforms" to the standard. Most importantly, the judge will have the exhibitor move the dog around the ring in some pattern that he should specify. Finally, the judge will give the dog one last look before moving on to the next exhibitor.

If you are not in the top four in your class at your first show, do not be discouraged. Be patient and consistent, and you may eventually find yourself in a winning line-up. Remember that the winners were once in your shoes and have devoted many hours and much money to earn the placement. If you find that your dog is losing every time and never getting a nod, it may be time to consider a different dog sport or to just enjoy your Hovawart as a pet. Parent clubs offer working trials and other events, such as agility, tracking, obedience and more, which may be of interest to the owner of a well-trained Hovawart.

for pure-bred dogs—should be bred. Altered dogs, however, can participate in other events such as obedience trials, flyball, agility and other performance events.

Before you actually step into the ring, you would be well advised to sit back and observe the judge's ring procedure. If it is your

FÉDÉRATION CYNOLOGIQUE INTERNATIONALE

Established in 1911, the Fédération Cynologique Internationale (FCI) represents the "world kennel club." This international body brings uniformity to the breeding, judging and showing of pure-bred dogs. Although the FCI originally included only five European nations: France, Germany, Austria, the Netherlands and Belgium (which remains its headquarters), the organization today embraces nations on six continents and recognizes well over 300 breeds of pure-bred dog.

The FCI sponsors both national and international shows. Dogs from every country can participate in these impressive canine spectacles, the largest of which is the World Dog Show, hosted in a different country each year. The hosting country determines the judging system and breed standards are always based on the breed's country of origin.

There are three titles attainable through the FCI: the International Champion, which is the most prestigious; the International Beauty Champion, which is based on aptitude certificates in different countries; and the International Trial Champion, which is based on achievement in obedience trials in different countries. An FCI title requires a dog to win three CACs (*Certificats d'Aptitude au Championnat*), at regional or club shows under three different judges who are breed specialists. The title of International Champion is gained by winning CACIBs (*Certificats d'Aptitude au Championnat International de Beauté*), which are offered only at international shows. The International Champion must have twice won the CACIB and—according to its nationality—be in possession of a SchH or RCI. One of the CACIBs must have been awarded in the country where the dog is registered, or in the country where the breed originated (in the case of the Hovawart, Germany). The other CACIB must have come from a second country.

The FCI breeds are divided into ten groups; the Hovawart competes in Group 2 with a working trial. There are various classes in which you can register your dog, depending on the dog's age.

FCI QUALIFIERS

- Fair: Dog is acceptable but without any particular qualities or special physical condition;
- Good: The dog possesses the characteristics of its breed but has faults that are not correctable;
- Very Good: The dog possesses the perfect characteristics of its breed and is in good physical condition but has some minor faults;
- Excellent: The dog approaches the standard of its breed, is in almost perfect condition and is balanced and happy.

HOVAWART

THINK LIKE A DOG

Dogs do not think like humans, nor do humans think like dogs, though we try. Unfortunately, a dog is incapable of comprehending how humans think, so the responsibility falls on the owner to adopt a viable canine mindset. Dogs cannot rationalize, and dogs exist in the present moment. Many a dog owner makes the mistake in training of thinking that he can reprimand his dog for something the dog did a while ago. Basically, you cannot even reprimand a dog for something he did 20 seconds ago! Either catch him in the act or forget it! It is a waste of your and your dog's time—in his mind, you are reprimanding him for whatever he is doing at that moment.

The following behavioral problems represent some which owners most commonly encounter. Every dog is unique and every situation is unique. No author could purport for you to solve your Hovawart's problems simply by reading a chapter in a book. Here we outline some basic "dogspeak" so that owners' chances of solving behavioral problems are increased. We hope that you will make a valiant effort to

solve your Hovawart's problems. Patience and understanding are virtues that must dwell in every pet-loving household.

SEPARATION ANXIETY

Recognized by behaviorists as the most common form of stress for dogs, separation anxiety can also lead to destructive behaviors in your dog. It's more than your Hovawart's howling his displeasure at your leaving the house and his being left alone. This is a normal reaction, no different from the child who cries as his mother leaves him on the first day at school. Separation anxiety is more serious. In fact, if you are constantly with your dog, he will come to expect you with him all of the time, making it even more traumatic for him when you are not there. Obviously, you enjoy spending time with your dog, and he thrives on your love and attention. However, it should not become a dependent relationship in which he is heartbroken without you.

One thing you can do to minimize separation anxiety is to make your entrances and exits as low-key as possible. Do not give your dog a long drawn-out goodbye, and do not lavish him with hugs and kisses when you return. This is giving in to the attention that he craves, and it will only make him miss it more when you are away. Another thing you can try is to give your dog a treat when you leave; this not only will keep him occupied and keep his mind off the fact that you have just left but also will help him associate your leaving with a pleasant experience.

You may have to accustom your dog to being left alone at intervals. Of course, when your dog starts whimpering as you approach the door, your first instinct will be to run to him and comfort him, but do not do it! Eventually he will adjust to your absence. His anxiety stems from being placed in an unfamiliar situation; by familiarizing him with being alone, he will learn that he will survive. That is not to say that you should purposely leave your dog home alone, but the dog needs to know that, while he can depend on you for his care, you do not have to be by his side 24 hours a day. Some behaviorists recommend tiring the dog out before you leave home—take him for a good long walk or engage in a game of fetch in the yard.

When the dog is alone in the house, he should be placed in his crate—another distinct advantage to crate-training your dog. The crate should be placed in his famil-iar happy family area, where he normally sleeps and already feels comfortable, thereby making him feel more at ease when he is alone. Be sure to give the dog a special chew toy to enjoy while he settles into his crate.

AGGRESSION

This is a problem that concerns all responsible dog owners. Aggression can be a very big problem in dogs, and, when not controlled, always becomes dangerous. An aggressive dog, no matter the size, may lunge at, bite or even attack a person or another dog. Aggressive behavior is not to be tolerated. It is more than just inappropriate behavior; it is painful for a family to watch their dog become unpredictable in his behavior to the point where they are afraid of him.

It is important not to challenge an aggressive dog, as this could provoke an attack. Observe your

"LONELY WOLF"
The number of dogs that suffer from separation anxiety is on the rise as more and more pet owners find themselves at work all day. New attention is being paid to this problem, which is especially hard to diagnose since it is only evident when the dog is alone. Research is currently being done to help educate dog owners about separation anxiety and how they can help minimize this problem in their dogs.

Hovawart's body language. Does he make direct eye contact and stare? Does he try to make himself as large as possible: ears pricked, chest out, tail erect? Height and size signify authority in a dog pack—being taller or "above" another dog literally means that he is "above" in social status. These body signals tell you that your Hovawart thinks he is in charge, a problem that needs to be addressed. An aggressive dog is unpredictable; you never know when he is going to strike and what he is going to do. You cannot understand why a dog that is playful one minute is growling the next.

Fear is a common cause of aggression in dogs. Perhaps your Hovawart had a negative experience as a puppy, which causes him to be fearful when a similar situation presents itself later in life. The dog may act aggressively in order to protect himself from whatever is making him afraid. It is not always easy to determine what is making your dog fearful, but if you can isolate what brings out the fear reaction, you can help the dog get over it.

Supervise your Hovawart's interactions with people and other dogs, and praise the dog when it goes well. If he starts to act aggressively in a situation, correct him and remove him from the situation. Do not let people approach the dog and start petting him without your express permission. That way, you can have the dog sit to accept petting, and praise him when he behaves properly. You are focusing on praise and on modifying his behavior by rewarding him when he acts appropriately. By being gentle and by supervising his interactions, you are showing him that there is no need to be afraid or defensive.

The best solution is to consult a behavioral specialist, one who has experience with large dogs or similar breeds if possible. Together, perhaps you can pinpoint the cause of your dog's aggression and do something about it. An aggressive dog cannot be trusted, and a dog that cannot be trusted is not safe to have as a family pet.

AGGRESSION TOWARD OTHER DOGS
A dog's aggressive behavior toward another dog stems from insufficient exposure to other dogs at an early age. If other dogs make your Hovawart nervous and agitated, he will lash out as a protective mechanism. The animal becomes so dominant that he does not even show signs that he is fearful or threatened. Without growling or any other physical signal as a warning, he will lunge at and bite the other dog.

A way to correct this is to let your Hovawart approach another dog when walking on lead. Watch very closely and, at the first sign of aggression, correct your Hovawart

When two dogs meet, they will usually sniff each other as an act of getting to know each other.

and pull him away. Scold him for any sign of discomfort, and then praise him when he ignores the other dog. Keep this up until either he stops the aggressive behavior, learns to ignore other dogs or even accepts other dogs. Praise him lavishly for this correct behavior.

DOMINANT AGGRESSION

A social hierarchy is firmly established in a wild dog pack. The dog wants to dominate those under him and please those above him. Dogs know that there must be a leader. If you are not the obvious choice for emperor, the dog will assume the throne! These conflicting innate desires are what a dog owner is up against when he sets about training a dog. In training a dog to obey commands, the owner is reinforcing that he is the top dog in the "pack" and that the dog should, and should want to, serve

his superior. Thus, the owner is suppressing the dog's urge to dominate by modifying his behavior and making him obedient.

An important part of training is taking every opportunity to reinforce that you are the leader. The simple action of making your Hovawart sit to wait for his food instead of allowing him to run up to get it when he wants it says that you control when he eats: he is dependent on you for food. Although it may be difficult, do not give in to your dog's wishes every time he whines at you or looks at you with pleading eyes. It is a constant effort to show the dog that his place in the pack is at the bottom. This is not meant to sound cruel or inhumane. You love your Hovawart and you should treat him with care and affection. You did not get a dog just so you could control another creature. Dog training is not about being cruel, it is about molding the dog's behavior into what is acceptable and teaching him to live by your rules. In theory, it is quite simple: catch him in appropriate behavior and reward him for it; catch him in a misdeed and correct him for it. Add a dog into the equation and it becomes a bit more trying, but as a rule of thumb, positive reinforcement is what works best.

With a dominant dog, punishment and negative reinforcement can have the opposite effect of what you are after. It can make a dog fearful and/or act out aggressively if he feels that he is being challenged. Remember, a dominant dog perceives himself at the top of the social heap and will fight to defend his perceived status. The best way to prevent that is to never give him reason to think that he is in control in the first place.

If you are having trouble training your Hovawart and it seems as if he is constantly challenging your authority, seek the help of an obedience trainer or behavioral specialist. A professional will work with both you and your dog to teach you effective techniques to use at home. Beware of trainers who rely on excessively harsh methods; scolding is necessary now and then, but the focus in your training should *always* be on positive reinforcement.

SEXUAL BEHAVIOR

To a certain extent, spaying/ neutering will eliminate sexual behaviors, but if you are purchasing a dog that you wish to breed from, you should be aware of what you will have to deal with.

Female dogs usually have two estruses per year, with each season lasting about three weeks. These are the only times in which a female dog will mate, and she usually will not allow this until the second week of the cycle, although this varies from bitch to bitch. If not bred during the heat cycle, it is not uncommon for a bitch to experience a false pregnancy, in which her mammary glands swell and she exhibits nesting behavior and maternal tendencies toward toys or other objects.

With male dogs, owners must be aware that whole dogs (dogs who are not neutered) have the natural inclination to mark their territory. Males mark their territory by spraying small amounts of urine as they lift their legs in a macho ritual. Marking can occur both outdoors in the yard and around

TUG-OF-WAR

You should never play tug-of-war games with your puppy. Such games create a struggle for "top dog" position and teach the puppy that it is okay to challenge you. It will also encourage your puppy's natural tendency to bite down hard and *win*.

the neighborhood as well as indoors on furniture legs, curtains and the sofa. Such behavior can be very frustrating for the owner; early training is strongly urged before the "urge" strikes your dog. Neutering the male at an appropriate early age can solve this problem before it becomes a habit.

Other problems associated with males are wandering and mounting, although a Hovawart is unlikely to stray too far from home. Both of these habits, of course, belong to the unneutered dog, whose sexual drive leads him away from home in search of the bitch in heat. Males will mount females in heat, as well as any other dog, male or female, that happens to catch their fancy. Other possible mounting partners include his owner, the furniture, guests to the home and strangers on the street. Discourage such behavior early on.

Owners must further recognize that mounting is not merely a sexual expression but also one of dominance, seen in both males and females alike. Be consistent and be persistent, and you will find that you can "move mounters."

CHEWING

The national canine pastime is chewing! Dogs need to chew to massage their gums, to make their new teeth feel better and to exercise their jaws. Your role as owner is not to stop the dog's chewing, but

rather to redirect it to positive, chew-worthy objects. Be an informed owner and purchase proper chew toys, like strong nylon bones, that will not splinter. Be sure that the objects are safe and durable, since your dog's safety is at risk. The owner is responsible for ensuring a dog-proof environment.

The best answer is prevention; that is, put your shoes, handbags and other objects out of the reach of the growing canine mouth. Direct your pup to his toys whenever you see him "tasting" the furniture legs or the leg of your pants. Make a loud noise to attract the pup's attention and immediately escort him to his chew toy and engage him with the toy for at least four minutes, praising and encouraging him all the while. An array of safe, interesting chew toys will keep your dog's mind and teeth occupied, and distracted from chewing on things he shouldn't.

Dog toys are made specifically to attract a dog's attention and to provide a proper outlet for his chewing. Always have safe toys available for your Hovawart puppy or adult.

An alert
protector of his
property, your
Hovawart will
sound the alarm
when he deems
necessary.

An alert protector of his property, your Hovawart will sound the alarm when he deems necessary.

Some trainers recommend deterrents, such as hot pepper, a bitter spice or a product designed for this purpose, to discourage the dog from chewing unwanted objects. Test these products to see which works best before investing in large quantities.

BARKING

Although not an excessive barker, the Hovawart has an imposing voice and physique that puts fear into any intruder. Therefore, if an intruder came into your home in the middle of the night and your Hovawart barked a warning, wouldn't you be pleased? You would probably deem your dog a hero, a wonderful guardian and protector of the home. On the other hand, if a friend drops by unexpectedly, rings the doorbell and is greeted with a sudden sharp bark, you would probably be annoyed at the dog. But in reality, isn't this just the same behavior? The dog does not know any better. Unless he sees who is at the door and it is someone he knows, he will bark as a means of vocalizing that his (and your) territory is being threatened. While your friend is not posing a threat, it is all the same to the dog. Barking is his means of letting you know that there is an intrusion, whether friend or foe, on your property. This type of barking is instinctive and should not be discouraged.

Excessive habitual barking, however, is a problem that should be corrected early on. As your Hovawart grows up, you will be able to tell when his barking is purposeful and when it is for no reason. You will become able to distinguish your dog's different barks and their meanings. For example, the bark when someone comes to the door will be different from the bark when he is excited to see you. It is similar to a person's tone of voice, except that the dog has to rely totally on tone of voice because he does not have the advantage of using words. An incessant barker will be evident at an early age.

There are some things that encourage a dog to bark. For example, if your dog barks non-stop for a few minutes and you give him a treat to quiet him, he believes that you are rewarding him for barking. He will associate barking with getting a treat and will keep doing it until he is rewarded. On the other hand, if you give him a command such as "Quiet" and praise him after he has stopped barking for a few seconds, he will get the idea that being "quiet" is what you want him to do.

JUMPING UP
Jumping up is a dog's friendly way of saying hello! Some dog owners do not mind when their dogs jump up. The problem arises when guests come to the house and the dog greets them in the same manner—whether they like it or not! However friendly the greeting may be, the chances are that your visitors will not appreciate your dog's enthusiasm. The dog will not be able to distinguish upon whom he can jump and whom he cannot. Therefore, it is best to discourage this behavior entirely.

Pick a command such as "Off" (avoid using "Down" since you will use that for the dog to lie down) and tell him "Off" when he jumps up. Place him on the ground on all fours and have him sit, praising him the whole time. Always lavish him with praise and petting when he is in the sit position. In this way, you can give him a warm affectionate greeting, let him know that you are as pleased to see him

NO JUMPING
Stop a dog from jumping up before he jumps. If he is getting ready to jump onto you, simply walk away. If he jumps up on you before you can turn away, lift your knee so that it bumps him in the chest. Do not be forceful. Your dog soon will realize that jumping up is not a productive way of getting attention.

as he is to see you and instill good manners at the same time!

DIGGING
Digging, which is seen as a destructive behavior to humans, is actually quite a natural behavior in dogs. Although terriers (the "earth dogs") are most associated with digging, any dog's desire to dig can be irrepressible and most frustrating to his owners. When digging occurs in your yard, it is actually a normal behavior redirected into something the dog can do in his everyday life. In the wild, a dog would be actively seeking food, making his own shelter, etc. He would be using his paws in a purposeful manner for his survival. Since you provide him with food and shelter, he has no need to use his paws for these purposes, and so the energy that he would be using may manifest itself in the form of little holes all over your yard and flower beds.

Perhaps your dog is digging as

a reaction to boredom—it is somewhat similar to someone eating a whole bag of chips in front of the TV—because they are there and there is nothing better to do! Basically, the answer is to provide the dog with adequate play and exercise so that his mind and paws are occupied, and so that he feels as if he is doing something useful.

Of course, digging is easiest to control if it is stopped as soon as possible, but it is often hard to catch a dog in the act. If your dog is a compulsive digger and is not easily distracted by other activities, you can designate an area on your property where he is allowed to dig. If you catch him digging in an off-limits area of the garden, immediately take him to the approved area and praise him for digging there. Keep a close eye on him so that you can catch him in the act—that is the only way to make him understand what is permitted and what is not. If you take him to a hole he dug an hour ago and tell him "No," he will understand that you are not fond of holes, dirt or flowers. If you catch him while he is stifle-deep in your tulips, that is when he will get your message.

FOOD STEALING

Is your dog devising ways of stealing food from your coffee table or kitchen counter? If so, you must answer the following questions: Is your Hovawart a bit hungry, or is he "constantly famished" like

many dogs seem to be? Face it, some dogs are more food-motivated than others. They are totally obsessed by the smell of food and can only think of their next meal. Food stealing is terrific fun and always yields a great reward— FOOD, glorious food.

Your goal as an owner, therefore, is to be sensible about where food is placed in the home and to reprimand your dog whenever he is caught in the act of stealing. But remember, only reprimand your dog if you actually see him stealing, not later when the crime is discovered; that will be of no use at all and will only serve to confuse the dog.

BEGGING

Just like food stealing, begging is a favorite pastime of hungry puppies! It achieves that same great result—FOOD! Dogs quickly learn that their owners keep the "good food" for themselves, and that we humans do not dine on dry food alone. Begging is a conditioned response related to a specific stimulus, time and place. The sounds of the kitchen, cans and bottles opening, crinkling bags, the smell of food in preparation, etc., will excite the dog, and soon the paws will be in the air!

Here is the solution to stopping this behavior: Never give in to a beggar! You are rewarding the dog for sitting pretty, jumping up, whining and rubbing his nose into you by giving him food. By ignoring the dog, you will (eventually) force the behavior into extinction. Note that the behavior is likely to get worse before it disappears, so be sure there are not any "softies" in the family who will give in to little "Oliver" every time he whimpers, "More, please."

COPROPHAGIA

Feces eating is, to humans, one of the most disgusting behaviors that their dogs could engage in; yet, to dogs, it is perfectly normal. It is hard for us to understand why a dog would want to eat his own feces. He could be seeking certain nutrients that are missing from his diet, he could be just hungry or he could be attracted by the pleasing (to a dog) scent. While coprophagia most often refers to the dog's eating his own feces, a dog may just as likely eat that of another animal as well if he comes across it. Dogs often find the stool of cats and horses more palatable than that of other dogs.

Vets have found that diets with low levels of digestibility, containing relatively low levels of fiber and high levels of starch, increase coprophagia. Therefore, high-fiber diets may decrease the likelihood of dogs' eating feces. Both the consistency of the stool (how firm it feels in the dog's mouth) and the presence of undigested nutrients increase the likelihood. Thus, once the dog develops diarrhea from feces eating, he will likely stop this distasteful habit.

To discourage this behavior, first make sure that the food you are feeding your dog is nutritionally complete and that he is getting enough food. If changes in his diet do not seem to work, and no medical cause can be found, you will have to modify the behavior through environmental control before it becomes a habit. The best way to prevent your dog from eating his stool is to make it unavailable—clean up after he eliminates and remove any stool from the yard. If it is not there, he cannot eat it.

Reprimanding for stool eating rarely impresses the dog. Vets recommend distracting the dog while he is in the act of stool eating. Coprophagia is seen most frequently in pups 6 to 12 months of age, and usually disappears around the dog's first birthday.

INDEX

Page numbers in **boldface** indicate illustrations.

My Hovawart

PUT YOUR PUPPY'S FIRST PICTURE HERE

Dog's Name _____

Date _____ Photographer _____